RECIPES
from
SWEET YESTERDAY
by
Thelma Allen

To Lill —
cooking is fun!
Thelma

RECIPES FROM SWEET YESTERDAY – Volume One
Thelma Allen

Second printing, November 1994
Third printing, November 1995
Fourth printing, March 1997
Fifth printing, May 1997
Sixth printing, July 1997
Seventh printing, August 1997
Eighth printing, November 1997
Ninth printing, February 2000
Tenth printing, December 2001

Published by:
Sweet Yesterday
P. O. Box 111510
Nashville, TN 37222

Author: Thelma Allen
Editors: Thelma Allen and Michael Allen
Graphic design/layout: Michael Allen
Illustrations: Sylvia Worcester
Cover photography: Michael Allen
Cover photograph models: Thelma Allen and her
        grandson, Allen Worcester
Cover photo stylists: Sylvia Worcester and
        Michael Allen
Kitchen in cover photograph furnished by Earl
        and Carrie Lannom
Typesetting: Debra Cummins
Electronic Prepress: McPherson and Kelley, Inc.
Printing: Harris Press, Inc.

ISBN 0-9668322-0-5

TABLE OF CONTENTS

DEDICATION

This book is dedicated to the memory of my mother and father, George and May Rogers, who were so ambitious for their children and worked so hard to obtain the best possible advantage in life for them. They were both born in Texas; my father in Hillsboro in 1883 and my mother in Kaufman in 1893. Their parents were from Kentucky and Mississippi. My father became both mother and father to us when my mother was killed in a tornado in 1928 in Blair, Oklahoma. I'm so grateful to my mother for the many things she taught us, thus we were able to maintain our home with the help of our father and stay together. My father died in Altus, Oklahoma, in 1953. My brother, who was so dear to us, also died in Altus in 1966. I'll always be thankful for the peaceful atmosphere my parents furnished us. We always knew we were loved, and they always had our best interest at heart. They never lectured us on how to live: they showed us. My father was one of those people whom the banker said "Your word is your bond." They both have been gone a long time, but death can not take away the pleasant memories or the principles of good morals they taught us that have been so rewarding to me in the building of my life and the life of my family. They taught us that happiness could only be obtained from living a good clean Christian life. Money can't buy that - no matter how much you have.

George and May Rogers

INTRODUCTION

My purpose for writing this book is to pass on to posterity the customs and habits that made up the life-styles of the pioneers - their farm life of work and play, especially the early years of my parents and family. I've preserved some of the cooking of the pioneer days, which is now history, for my family; a history that is so far removed from our present day living. I've tried to give you some of the old recipes that if not recorded will be lost forever. I don't believe there is anything that you can't buy as a mix; rarely is anything made from scratch.

How many times have I wished I knew more about my parents' early childhood, and there is nobody to ask. Both parents were from large families, and they are all gone except for 1 aunt. I lost both parents while still in my thirties. I'm the oldest living of all my cousins, and by reading my recipes you will notice that I have outlived many of my friends.

I hope our children, Mike and Sylvia, will pass on to future generations some of the history of their lives that is so different from the people and period that I have written about. Mike lives in Nashville, Tennessee, and has helped me tremendously in the design, cover photography and editing of the book. Sylvia resides in Oklahoma City with her husband, Gary Worcester, and has helped me with research and illustrations. Cooking is not Sylvia's cup of tea, but making life easier for her busy husband, a cardiologist, and rearing their son, Allen, is her whole purpose in life.

We lived in an era when life for everyone was hard. There were so many things that we had no control over, such as the Depression days, but the Depression probably made us stronger people in life's trials and tribulations.

My mother saw my sister, Marie, and me graduate from the 8th grade. Due to birthdays and convenience we were in the same grade. Soon after graduation I remember my mother telling us she didn't think she was going to live very long and wanted us to go to school as far as we could, work hard and "be somebody." Two weeks later she was killed in a tornado. That conversation is so vivid in my mind that it seems like yesterday. There was no way we could go to college - no grants, scholarships or student loans. I've always felt we were victims of the times, but we didn't allow it to make us bitter. Perhaps, it made us try harder.

I have always loved people and been of an accommodating nature. I have lived by the principle that you aren't living if you don't contribute something to humanity, even if it is a small bit. This idea has enriched my life "a hundredfold," and I hope the lives of the people around me.

I feel like a millionare when I can go to bed at night with clean sheets in a modest, comfortable home where the roof doesn't leak, and where I can be warm in the winter and cool in the summer. All the conveniences and neccesseties like central heating and cooling and machines that wash and dry our clothes seem like luxuries compared to the pioneer days. Even more exciting is to look out the door and see the many beautiful things God has created for us because He loves us.

Even though I was featured in an article in the March 1991 issue of "Good Housekeeping" magazine, I've never been famous, gone to college, or traveled abroad, but I've had a zest for living and lived with enthusiasm.

Some of the things I have done: sent 2 kids to college, a member of the same Church of Christ congregation for 60 years where I taught Sunday school and a licensed hairdresser for over 50 years. After retiring from the beauty shop, I started a new career, a craft business called "Sweet Yesterday", where I create my own products: quilted items, aprons, tote bags, etc.

I don't believe the "world owes me a living." I hope always to be on the tax roll - not the welfare roll. Perhaps this cookbook will help keep me on the tax rolls.

You will learn about my married life and the things my husband, Marvin, and I have done with our lives in my next cookbook.

A very special thanks to my family: my children, my husband (who has washed a lot of dishes, run the sweeper, and many other household duties) and my sister, for their support in this effort.

Also a very special thanks to Mabel Brown (86 years old) and Mary Loucyle Self (94 years old) who helped me with the old recipes and old time cooking procedures and to Olevia Robinson for her recipes and typing skills.

Thanks to all the people who gave me recipes with their names, and those who gave me their recipes without their names.

I know you will enjoy the recipes, pioneer history, philosophy, and helpful information in the cookbook. I have enjoyed doing it for you.

THELMA ALLEN

5

PORK

SOME PIONEER HISTORY

I was born on a farm in Palo Pinto County, Texas, in 1914, to George and May Rogers, nee Bonds. I had one half brother, Charlie Rogers, seven years older than I, whose mother died from childbirth and I have one sister, Marie who is 15 months younger than I. We knew he was our half brother, but we really grew up as full brother and sisters. Charlie was so good to us and made our life more interesting.

The life was hard, but we didn't know the difference and never complained. We did, however, welcome a rain so we could rest from picking or chopping cotton, or planting a garden, or the many other things that had to be done - like wash day.

WASH DAY

The wash day was a long one. The day before, the water was drawn for 3 tubs placed on a homemade bench. The wash pot in which we boiled the white clothes in was also readied. In the first tub we had cold water where we rubbed the white clothes on the washboard with lye soap. We used cold water in order not to set the dirt in the clothes. Next, the clothes were placed in the wash pot to boil for 15 to 20 minutes after the boiling water had been broken with lye (to make the water softer) and skimmed. We used slivered lye soap in the boiling water. My sister and I would take turns punching them with a stick, usually made from a broom handle. After boiling in the wash pot and using lye soap, the clothes went back to rinse in the first tub to which clean water was added. After this rinse they were rinsed again in the second tub. Next, the clothes were rinsed for another time in the third tub where a few drops of bluing were added. This solution helped take the yellow out of the clothes. Some young people today may wonder why you used something called "bluing" to help take the "yellow" out of clothes to make them "whiter". These steps were repeated with each additional load of white clothes.

Everybody prided themselves with white clothes. When white clothes were on the line, people would comment that someone did a "pretty" laundry.

You finished all the white clothes except for starching before you started the colored clothes. These clothes were done by the same method, except they were not boiled. They were rubbed in the first rinse water used for the white clothes that had been lifted from the boiling pot. By this time the water was hot enough to clean the colored clothes. The real dirty ones, like the mens' work clothes, were boiled. After the colored clothes were washed, we were ready to starch.

The starch was made by mixing flour and a quart of cold water into a paste in a large cooking kettle and gradually adding boiling water from a big tea kettle, stirring constantly. This mixture had to be boiled a few seconds to make sure the flour was cooked. Now it's ready to use after being strained through a flour sack to get the lumps out. The washboard by today's standard could be called a relic of babarism. Thank goodness there's no wash day on our weekly calendar now.

When the washing was finished, the soap suds were used to scrub the floors. The cleanest rinse water was left in the tub for baths. The water was either heated on the cook stove during winter or left out in the sun during the summer. During the summer months we would bathe outside in the dark.

There were no clothes dryers back then. In the winter when the weather was bad, the wet clothes were hung on the back of cane-bottom chairs inside. Clothes lines were hung all over the house, and the clothes were dried by heat from the wood stove in the front room. I can recall hanging clothes outside that would freeze by the time you got them on the line. We would put a jar of hot water or a heated rock in the clothes pin bag to keep our hands warm as we hung out the clothes. Our parents were certainly creative and inventive. We would also hang the clothes on fences and trees and hope they didn't get relocated by the wind. By late afternoon the clothes were dry and folded, or sprinkled by hand, folded in a sheet and ready to be ironed the next day. Some new products came later that were most welcomed, such as a clothes sprinkler and a wringer that operated by turning a crank.

IRONING

The ironing day in summer wasn't much fun, because we had to heat the irons on the wood stove. Cooking in those days was not that big of a problem, because the stove was hot to heat the irons, and my sister and I made cornbread. The rest of the food was cooked at breakfast time.

The first irons were one piece and were called "flat irons." When these irons got hot, you had to handle them with a cloth, but the ones I remember had a detachable wooden handle. We heated three irons at a time and covered them with a iron skillet (upside down) to keep them hot. Later, my father bought a gasoline iron. We still scorched the clothes because the heat couldn't be regulated, but we just wet the spot and put it in the sun. Then the scorched spot would disappear. Later, we bought an electric iron that was not heat-controlled either. You could mop the kitchen after you plugged in the iron. It took that long for the iron to heat. When it got too hot, you just unplugged it. When it was too cold, you just plugged it in again. It was a real improvement; at least we didn't get a headache from the fumes of the gasoline iron.

We ironed everything we could on what we called our eating table. We did the ironing on top of an old quilt and sheet placed at the end of the table. For the dresses and shirts, we had a homemade ironing board. The straight end sat on the eating table, and the pointed end sat on a chair back. We covered it with an old quilt and the best part of a (washed) cotton picking sack. The "ever'day" work clothes were not ironed, but my father and brother had ironed clothes to wear to town. They only had one pair of Sunday pants at a time. They were folded with legs together and put between mattresses (every bed had two mattresses) to keep the press.

As the clothes were ironed, they were put on homemade hangers made from a rolled "Farm and Ranch" magazine with a string tied with a loop in the center. There were no closets to hang clothes, so they were hung on a broomstick rod behind a curtain that was stretched in a corner of a room. The rod opened on one end so the loops could be slipped on and off.

Dinner (noon time) on wash day was cooked in a dutch oven (cast iron) in the coals where the clothes had been boiled. The bread for the noon meal was cooked at breakfast. The meal was usually potatoes, dried beans or peas, and cornbread. During the spring and summer, fresh vegetables from the garden would be on the table. Corn, or

10

"roasting" ears as we called them, were often cooked on wash day. We stripped the shucks off the fresh gathered corn nearly to the end, cut off the tips with scissors and removed the silks with a brush or a soft cloth. The ears were then dipped in cold water, and the shucks were put back in place. The ears were fitted snugly in a Dutch oven and cooked over the fire for 30 to 35 minutes. You could also fry cornbread on the wash day fire. Needless to say, the meal was good, and we were hungry. I don't remember anyone saying "I don't like this". If we had, our father would have said, "You eat what your mother fixed for you".

HOG KILLING DAY

The most productive day of the year was when we killed the hogs. The weather has to be cold, late fall or winter, so we could hang the meat in the smokehouse without spoiling. We usually killed about four hogs. It was a long day that started at daylight and lasted until midnight. Preparation was started the day before. Trenches were dug and readied for the fire. The vats were cleaned and made ready to boil the water. The water had also been carried to the scene in milk buckets, tubs, cream cans, or anything else we could find that would hold water. The wood to heat the water was also in place. Then the hogs were ready to be killed, scalded and hung.

The hogs were killed two at a time with a blow to the head with a single-bladed axe. The next step was to scald them and then hang them to a "single tree" hoisted up the gatepost in the cow lot. The "single tree" was the implement that you used to hook a single animal to a plow or buggy. The purpose for hanging the hog was to let him bleed after the throat was slit and to remove the entrails.

Large sharp knives were used to scrape the hairs off the hogs after they were put in the wagon from the gatepost. The sideboards were removed for easy access to the bed. The hogs were cut into shoulders, ham, bacon, ribs, backbone, meat for sausage, and the organs were removed, such as the hearts, brains and livers. Some of the fat that was easily removed was put in a big wash pot to render into lard. The ham, shoulder, and bacon were salt-cured. The heart, liver, brains and some pieces that weren't cured were divided with the neighbors that helped on this eventful day.

My father and brother carried slop, water and shelled corn to feed those critters from birth to killing day. My sister and I even rode the big sows. We had mixed emotions about killing them, but we had only chickens to eat during the summer and were glad to have the change. Occasionally, someone would kill a beef and would peddle it to the neighbors. It was a welcome change, too.

The women would help my mother with taking off the fat from the entrails and other places. The leaf lard came from ribs and stomach. Liver and onions were fried for dinner (noon time) the first day of hog killing. There were also potatoes in a cream sauce and always plenty of hot bread. The table always had a big bowl of butter in the middle. The meal was "topped off" with plenty of slices of molasses pye. Pie was spelled with a "y" in the 1800's.

MOLASSES PYE
used by my grandmother - Ollie Rogers

3 eggs
1 cup sugar
1 cup molasses
1/2 cup melted butter
1 tsp. vanilla
1 pie shell (9 inch, unbaked)

Beat molasses until light. Add sugar and beat again. Then add molasses, butter and vanilla. Place in a 9 inch pie pan. Bake about 10 minutes in hot oven. Reduce heat by not adding wood. Bake until custard is set.

We were in the process of grinding sausage by suppertime, and sausage was fried for supper to test the seasoning. This testing was done several times before putting sausage in sacks to hang. The sacks were long tubes made from the best parts of old sheets or flour sacks. The sacks were tied, gathered at the top with binder twine, and hung in the smokehouse. Some of the fried sausage was put into big fruit jars and crocks covered with lard that made a good sealer. Lids were placed on the jars, and the crocks were covered with several squares of cheesecloth or any clean cloth that could be wrapped around and tied.

We had tenderloin with cream gravy the morning after the killing. The second morning for breakfast we had scrambled eggs with brains. We didn't like the idea of eating brains, but we were told it would make us smarter. So we ate them.

The work was not finished the first day. My mother, sister and I rendered the lard, cooked the head for mincemeat, and rendered the rinds for soap grease. If we didn't get the rinds too brown, they were put into cracklin' bread or eaten as snacks.

The hog and it's by-products meant as much to us as the buffalo meant to the survival of the Indians.

I wish I could give you my mother's recipe for lye soap, but she didn't have one. She did make it in the wash pot and used soap grease rendered from the hog and cracklings. This recipe is similar to the way she made soap.

LYE SOAP

6 lbs. clean fat, tallow, pure lard, or
     strained bacon drippings
1 can (12 oz.) lye
2 1/2 pints water

In enamel, cast iron or steel container, slowly add lye to cold water. Stir to dissolve with wooden spoon. Melt fat and let cool to 85°. Pour lye solution into melted fat in a thin, steady stream with slow, even stirs. Keep stirring until wooden spoon will stand alone in mixture. When all the lye is blended in the fat, pour into pasteboard box or wooden box lined with brown paper. Remove and cut into bars. Keep dry at room temperature to cure for about 2 weeks.

My mother used hot water, and cooked the soap in the wash pot. She cut the soap into bars and put them in boxes to dry.

"It is better to dwell in the wilderness, than with a contentious and an angry woman."
Proverbs 21:19

14

MINCEMEAT

3 lbs. lean meat from hog head (cooked
    and chopped)
6 lbs. apples (peeled, seeded and
    chopped)
1 cup vinegar
2 quarts apple cider
1/4 cup lemon juice
1 cup orange juice
1 1/2 cup molasses
3 cups sugar
4 lbs. raisins (seeded)
2 lbs. apricots (dried)
1 cup fruit juice (such as canned
    peaches or peach pickle juice)
2 lbs. currants
3 tsp. nutmeg
3 tsp. cloves
2 tsp. allspice
4 Tbsp. cinnamon
2 Tbsp. salt
3 quarts water

Cook meat until tender for about 30
minutes in enough water to cover. Let
stand for a few hours. Add apples,
raisins, dried apricots and currants.
Dried peaches may be added. Add rest
of the ingredients and cook slowly for 2
hours in open kettle. Seal while hot.
Will make about 12 pints. Can store in
refrigerator indefinitely. If using a pint
for a pie, I like to add a can of
pineapple. Makes 2 pies. If using
pineapple, you will need to add about 2
Tbsp. of flour or cornstarch.

SALT CURED HAM

After washing the ham thoroughly to get the mold off, soak in cold water for 24 hours. Then wash again. Place the ham back in the pot and cover with cold water and add 1 cup of vinegar. My father used a black iron wash pot and cooked outside. Peach pickle juice may be added. Bring to a boil and simmer for 15 to 20 minutes per lb. Ham should be done. Do not boil. Remove from heat and let it cool in the liquid where it was cooked. Take off skin. If there is too much fat, take off excess and save to season vegetables. Score remaining fat and place in pan, fat side up with a cup or more of ham liquid. Bake about 1 hour. Baste with liquid so fat doesn't dry out. You can make a paste of prepared mustard, 1 1/4 cup brown sugar and 1/4 cup apple or orange juice. Spread on ham and bake slowly for another hour. Save the liquid from the second boiling. Put in smokehouse in coffee cans. It will freeze, and you can use in vegetables. Good in beans and black-eyed peas.

CRACKLIN' BREAD

2 cups cracklin' (made from rendering
            lard)
1 tsp. salt
2 cups corn meal
hot water

Cube cracklin' in small pieces and pour salt over them. Add enough hot water to make a stiff paste. Divide into oblong loaves and bake at 400° for 30 minutes.

SALT PORK WITH CREAM GRAVY
(cooked in a fireplace)
circa 1860

3/4 lb. salt pork
4 Tbsp. flour
2 1/4 cups milk
3/4 cup cream
1 Tbsp. bacon dripping or lard

Slice bacon in 1/8" strips. Pour hot milk on bacon, let set for 10 minutes. Take bacon out of milk and roll in enough flour to coat. Spread in a large spider (a large iron skillet with long handles and four legs) and place at the side of the fire until the fat is well fried out. Then draw gradually forward until slices begin to color. Transfer them to a heated platter and keep hot. Pour off most of the fat, leaving 2 Tbsp. in pan. Stir milk and cream into this mixture and when it comes to the boiling point, thicken slightly with flour blended with a little cold milk. Season with salt and pepper, boil up once and pour over pork.

KITCHEN KAPERS: Why don't we serve just plain food sometimes; I'd say most of the time. Most of us try to do that after Christmas Holiday dinners, but why wouldn't we enjoy them more often? Especially, since so many people eat their noon meal out. Pinto beans or black-eyed peas cooked with a pound of good sausage balls, instead of salt pork, and a glass bowl of chow chow on the side would be good. Don't forget the cornbread and green or sweet onions.

17

BARBECUED RIBS

2 lbs. pork ribs
1/2 cup vinegar
2 Tbsp. brown sugar
1/2 cup catsup
1 tsp. dry mustard
1/8 tsp. salt
1/4 cup lemon juice
2 Tbsp. Worchestershire sauce
1 tsp. paprika
1 onion (chopped)

Simmer all ingredients for 15 minutes. Pour over 2 lbs. of ribs and bake for 15 minutes at 450°   then at 350° for 1 1/2 hours.

PORK CHOPS WITH SPANISH RICE

1 1/2 lbs. pork chops
1 onion (chopped)
1 cup celery (chopped)
1/2 cup bell peppers
1 can (15 oz.) tomatoes
1 cup water
2 tsp. salt
1 tsp. paprika
2 tsp. sugar
1 cup raw rice

Brown meat in heavy skillet. Grease may not be needed if there is some fat on the meat. Add all ingredients except rice. Cover and cook slowly for about 20 minutes. Add rice and cook another 30 minutes (simmer) until rice is done. Serve hot.

SOUTHERN-STYLE PORK CHOPS
WITH RICE

6 thick pork chops
2/3 cup rice
1 cup water
2 tsp. salt
1/2 cup onions (chopped)
1 can tomatoes - 16 oz. (chopped)
1 cup whole kernel corn
1/4 tsp. pepper

Trim fat from pork chops and render in a large skillet. Brown chops in fat gradually and remove from skillet. Pour off excess fat. Spread rice in skillet and add water. Sprinkle with 1 tsp. salt. Arrange chops over rice. Sprinkle with remaining salt. Add onion and tomatoes and spoon on corn. Sprinkle with pepper and bring to a boil. Reduce heat, cover and simmer for 35 minutes. Add water, if necessary. Serves 6.

PORK CHOPS CREOLE

6 thick pork chops
1/4 cup cooking oil
1 clove of garlic (finely chopped)
1/2 cup green pepper (chopped)
1 small onion (chopped)
4 med fresh peeled tomatoes (chopped)
1/2 tsp. thyme
1 tsp. salt
pepper

Brown pork chops lightly in 2 Tbsp. of oil in large skillet. Saute` garlic, green pepper and onion in 2 Tbsp. of oil in small skillet. Add tomatoes, thyme, salt and pepper. Add pork chops to sauce. Steam and cover for 30 minutes or until tender. Serves 6.

PORK ROAST WITH VEGETABLES

1 pork roast (4 lbs.)
salt
2 cups chopped onions
6 large potatoes
2 cans (15 oz.) lima beans
2 cans (15 oz.) peas
1 large can green beans
pepper to taste
1 cup barbeque sauce

Rub roast with salt and place in a large pan on bottom rack of oven. Bake at 350° for 3 hours. Combine onions, potatoes, beans, peas, green beans, salt to taste and pepper. Cook until potatoes are tender. Slice roast into 1/2 inch slices and cover evenly with vegetables. Pour sauce over vegetables and spread out evenly. Bake for 30 minutes more. Will serve 12.

HERBED PORK CHOPS

6 loin pork chops
2 Tbsp. flour
1 tsp. salt
dash of pepper
1 can cream of mushroom soup
1/4 tsp. rosemary (crushed)
1 can French–fried onion rings
1/2 cup sour cream

Trim excess fat from chops. Place excess fat in skillet and render until 2 Tbsp. of fat collects in skillet. Remove trimmings. Mix flour, salt and pepper. Dredge chops in seasoned flour. Brown in hot fat and place in shallow baking dish. Combine soup, 3/4 cup of water and rosemary. Pour over chops and

20

sprinkle with half the onion rings. Cover and bake at 350° for 50 minutes or until pork is tender. Uncover and sprinkle with remaining onion rings. Bake for 10 minutes longer. Remove pork to platter. Blend sour cream into soup mixture in saucepan and heat through. Serve gravy with pork. Set six places at the dinnertable.

SPARERIBS AND SAUERKRAUT

3 lbs. spareribs, cut in 2-rib pieces
1 can sauerkraut (1 lb., 11 oz.)
1/2 cup onions (chopped)
1/4 tsp. marjoram
2 tsp. sugar
1 tsp. salt
1/4 tsp. pepper

Arrange ribs with rib ends down in 13 x 9 inch baking dish. Cover and bake at 325° for 1 hour and 30 minutes. Pour off drippings. Remove spareribs. Combine sauerkraut, onions, marjoram and sugar in baking dish. Arrange spareribs with brownside up on top of sauerkraut mixture and season with salt and pepper. Bake uncovered for 45 minutes or until spareribs are tender. Serves 4-6.

POULTRY

It's hard for us to imagine the limitations of our great-great-grandmothers as they prepared the first Thanksgiving dinner in the New World. Of course, they had the native American wild turkey in abundant quantities. They did not have sugar or coffee. Sugar was known as a condiment, like cloves and cinnamon are today. Coffee would not be introduced in England for another 30 years after the pilgrims landed on Plymouth Rock. The art of preserving by sealing cans and refrigeration was over 200 years in the future.

What would we do today if there were no supermarkets?

Other than my early day training by my mother, Mrs. Mills (my sister's mother-in-law) inspired and taught me more than anybody in the art of cooking. Since we were without a mother, we went to her for help in the kitchen. She was such as delightful person and loved to cook and entertain. That's the reason for using so many of her wonderful recipes in my cookbook. They are in the possession of my sister, Marie Mills, who is also an excellent cook. We are both thankful that Mrs. Mills taught us a lot about cooking.

Mrs. Mills received a B. S. degree from East Texas State Teachers College in 1898. Back at the turn of the century, not a lot of farm girls in Texas like Mrs. Mills went to college and became teachers. Mrs. Mills and her husband, who was also a teacher, went into farming full time.

The first turkey I ever cooked was for Thanksgiving dinner in the third year of my marriage and was Mrs. Mills' recipe. Her husband was dying in the hospital, and I took a plate of my first turkey dinner to her at the hospital. She never stopped talking about that turkey as long as she lived.

MRS. MILLS' ROAST TURKEY
AND DRESSING
circa 1935

Before placing on a rack in an open roaster, cover the turkey with a paste. Cream together 1/4 cup of soft butter (not melted), 5 Tbsp. of flour, and 2 Tbsp. of lemon juice. This will look like whipped cream. Put heavy coating of this paste over the wings, breast and thigh joints. Also put a thin coating over the rest of the body. This will allow the turkey to brown nicely and be tender and moist.

DRESSING - This recipe makes a lot, so you can freeze some.

6 cups of cornbread
4 cups of stale whitebread
        (I use hamburger buns left out
        for a day to dry)
1 to 1/2 cups celery (chopped)
1 to 1/2 cups onions (chopped)
1 tsp. thyme
4 Tbsp. sage
4 eggs (beaten)
1 cup melted butter or oleo
pepper to taste

Steam onions and celery in butter in iron skillet. Do not brown. Crumble the bread mixture into bite sizes. Mix the bread crumbs with the seasoning and set overnight. Next morning, steam celery and onions, and add to bread mixture. Add a small amount of hot broth to moisten, then add melted butter and beaten eggs. Add more hot broth -- just enough to make a dressing that will hold together. Press a handful of mixture into a ball that will hold together in your hand, but will break apart as falls onto a plate. Then I know it has enough moisture to bake. Let it stand a few minutes. Add more broth if you think it needs it. Put in pan, well-greased, bake at 375° until done. Don't overcook.

GIBLET GRAVY

Pour off all fat from roaster. Measure 4 Tbsp. of fat and return to roaster. Add 4 Tbsp. of flour which has been made into paste by adding a little cold water. Cook and brown well. Scrape all crustiness from sides of roaster. Cook flour well, but do not scorch. Use low heat. Add 2 cups of turkey broth. If you don't have 2 cups, finish with water. Cook until smooth and thickened. Add chopped liver and gizzard. Some like chopped hard-cooked eggs. By this time you may want to take a shortcut and use a can of cream of chicken soup diluted with a little milk. It makes a good gravy. You can add the giblets now.

MRS. MILLS' CHICKEN CROQUETTES
circa 1918

Make a sauce with 4 Tbsp. of butter, 6 Tbsp. of flour and 1 cup of milk, seasoned with salt, parsley and lemon juice. Cook 1 pint of cut chicken and spread on platter to cool. When cool, shape into cutlets or cone shape. Roll in bread crumbs, then in beaten eggs and roll again in crumbs. Fry in hot fat. Serve in mushroom sauce or Bechamel sauce.

Mushroom sauce is made by adding 1 Tbsp. of lemon juice to 1 cup of cream sauce an 1/2 cup of cooked mushrooms, cut into pieces.

Bechamel sauce is make like white sauce with clear stock and cream, instead of milk. One whole egg or 2 beaten yolks are added just before serving.

My mother started using this recipe around 1912. I have used it for most of my married life.

ROAST TURKEY OR HEN
circa 1912

A cloth (flour sack) brushed with shortening keeps the bird moist during roasting. It's a no-baste procedure. Wash, clean and dry bird really well. Brush bird with melted shortening and cover with cloth brushed with melted shortening. Leave cloth on during roasting. Roast the bird in moderate oven (350°) allowing 20 to 25 minutes per lb. Turn during later part of roasting to brown bird uniformly all over. Let cool for a few minutes and then carve on a warm platter.

26

The chicken contributed a lot to our limited menu. We raised our own. We ordered a hundred baby chicks at a time from a hatchery in Waxahachie, Texas, and picked them up at the train depot on the same day they were shipped. In the cellar there was an incubator we called the "The Little Red Hen" that could hatch a hundred eggs. The eggs had to be turned every day. As soon as we could tell the gender, we began eating the roosters, saving the others for egg production. When the roosters got too old to fry or bake, they were boiled and made into "scrapple."

My mother could walk out to the chicken yard and snag a chicken by using a hooked wire to catch the foot of the chicken "in nothing flat." The young ones were fried and served with cream gravy and hot biscuits, and the hens were boiled and the broth made a large pot of dumplings.

This is the way my mother made dumplings. Everybody made them this way. Drop dumplings were unheard of. This is the way I've made them since I've been cooking.

OLD TIME ROLLED DUMPLINGS

2 cups flour
2 Tbsp. lard (leveled)
1 egg (beaten in 3/4 cup of milk)
1/2 tsp. salt

Put salt and flour in mixing bowl, add shortening and blend as for biscuit dough. When mixed, add beaten egg and milk mixture, gradually, until it forms a real stiff dough. Divide into 3 parts, roll each part very thin on a heavily floured board. Cut into strips about 2 1/2 inches wide and 2 to 3 inches long.

When all have been cut, drop one at a time into briskly boiling broth. Beef or chicken broth will be fine. Some use backbone (pork) for dumplings. Have liquid boiling all the time while dropping in dough strips. Boil for 10 minutes or longer, depending how tender you like them. Stir constantly to keep from sticking. If you need a richer broth, add bouillon cubes or cream of chicken soup. You haven't lived until you have eaten these old time rolled dumplings.

MRS. MILLS' SCRAPPLE

Select 3 lbs. of chicken. Simmer in 3 quarts of water until the meat drops from the bone. Strain off the broth and remove the bone, taking care to get all the tiny pieces. Chop the meat into fine pieces. There should be about 2 quarts of liquid, and if necessary, add slowly enough water to make this quantity. Bring the broth to boiling point and slowly add 2 quarts of corn meal. Cook this mixture until it is a thick mush, stirring constantly. Add the chopped meat, salt and any seasoning desired, such as onion juice, sage, black pepper and thyme. Put the hot scrapple into an oblong pan that has been rinsed in cold water. Let stand until cold and firm. Slice and brown in a hot iron skillet. If the scrapple is rich with fat, no more fat is needed for frying. You could refrigerate now to make it easy to slice.

CHICKEN ALMONDINE
Olevia Robinson

2 cups of cooked chicken (diced)
1 small onion (minced)
6 Tbsp. butter
1/2 tsp. curry powder
dash of paprika
6 Tbsp. flour
1 can cream of chicken soup
2 cups milk
1/2 lb. cheddar cheese (grated)
1 cup blanched slivered almonds
  (toasted)
1 cup cooked rice
1 can (8 oz.) mushrooms (sliced)
buttered crumbs

Saute` onion in butter and blend in curry powder, paprika and flour. Blend soup and milk and stir into flour mixture. Cook over low heat, stirring constantly until smooth and thickened. Add cheese, stirring until melted. Fold in chicken, almonds, rice and mushrooms, mixing lightly. Pour into greased oblong baking dish and top with crumbs. Cover and bake at 325° for 20 minutes. Uncover and bake for an additional 25 minutes. Serves 8-10.

KITCHEN KAPERS: Did you ever wonder why Southern cooking is thought to be so good? Could it be the unlimited amount of cream, butter, fresh eggs, and the cool fresh buttermilk that was used for those flaky biscuits? There is nothing better to fry chicken in than lard mixed with some butter.

SYLVIA WORCESTER'S SOUTHERN FRIED CHICKEN

2 1/2 lbs. young frying chicken (cut up
        with skin removed)
2 cups flour
salt to taste
black pepper to taste
oregano or Fines Herbs
vegetable oil

Put flour in a large mixing bowl. Press the chicken pieces one at a time into the flour, being careful not to have any broken pieces in the coating. Place coated chicken into hot vegetable oil. Sprinkle salt, pepper and oregano (or Fines Herbs) on chicken. Turn chicken when crust is sealed and add more salt, pepper and oregano. When second side is sealed, reduce heat. Cook chicken slowly and turn several times, adding more seasoning, especially oregano, if necessary. When chicken is tender, remove from skillet and drain on several layers of paper towel. Tastes best when eaten while still hot.

MARIE MILLS' CHICKEN
IN GOLDEN SAUCE

2 lbs. chicken parts
1/2 cup flour
1/2 tsp. paprika
1/2 tsp. salt
1/4 cup butter (melted) or margarine
1 can (10 1/2 oz.) cream of chicken
        soup or mushroom soup
1/2 cup milk
1 Tbsp. parsley (minced)

Coat chicken with mixture of flour, paprika, salt and pepper. Arrange chicken in a single layer (skin down) in a buttered shallow baking dish 12 x 7 1/2 x 2 inches. Drizzle melted butter over chicken. Bake at 375° for 20 minutes. Turn chicken, bake 20 minutes longer. Mix soup and milk. Heat over slow heat, pour over chicken. Sprinkle parsley on top. Bake an additional 20 minutes.

DEE STEPHENS' CHICKEN
DRESSING CASSEROLE
my husband's niece

whole chicken or 4 breasts (stewed and
        boned, save broth)
10 oz. Pepperidge Farm dressing mix
1 can cream of celery soup
1 can cheddar cheese soup
1 small carton sour cream
1 bunch fresh green onions with tops
        added (chopped)
celery (chopped) added to dressing mix

Mix 3/4 of dressing mix with broth to thick consistency to spread evenly in 9 x 13 inch greased pan. Layer chicken on top of dressing. Pour mixture of soups, cream, onions and chopped celery over chicken. Sprinkle layer of dry dressing over top. Dot with oleo margarine. Bake at 350° for 30 minutes or until bubbly.

SHAKE AND BAKE CHICKEN

1 whole chicken (cut up) or breasts if preferred
2 cups dry bread crumbs (very fine) or 2 cups crackers
1/4 cup flour
2 tsp. sugar
2 tsp. oregano
2 tsp. garlic powder
2 Tbsp. paprika
2 Tbsp. onion powder
4 tsp. salt or less
1/2 cup shortening to fry in
3/4 cup milk

Mix ingredients well. Dip chicken in milk. Then into this mixture. Coat it well. Arrange in single layer in broiler pan. Bake at 400° for 40 to 60 minutes. When brown on one side, turn and brown on other side.

SHIRLEY CAUGHRAN'S CHRISPY OVEN-BAKED CHICKEN

my husband's niece

Combine 1/2 cup soy sauce with 2 Tbsp. oil and 1 clove of garlic (minced). Arrange cut pieces from 3 to 3 1/2 lbs. of broiler fryer in a flat shallow dish. Pour soy mixture over chicken and let stand about 30 minutes. Turn chicken pieces several times to coat all sides. Mix together: 1/2 cup wheat germ, 1/4 cup fine dry bread crumbs, 2 Tbsp. each sesame seeds and chopped parsley, 1/2 tsp. each paprika and pepper. Lift pieces from marinade, drain briefly, then turn in wheat germ mixture to evenly coat all sides. Shake off excess crumbs. Arrange coated chicken on well greased baking sheet. Bake uncovered at 350° for 1 hour or longer.

KITCHEN KAPERS: The best way to preserve garlic. First peel the garlic and break the buds apart. Take a jar with tight sealing lid, and after putting garlic into it, cover it completely with cooking oil. It will keep indefinitely and will always be ready to use. The oil will be very garlicky in just a few days. As the oil is used, just add more from time to time.

BEEF

In the pioneer days, everybody killed hogs, but beef was rarely butchered. Occasionally, someone would butcher a cow and peddle it in the neighborhood.

It was a real change from poultry and pork. During the Depression Days, the government paid the farmers to kill their cattle. Due to draught there was a shortage of feed, and due to the economy there was no money to buy feed. The farmers were not allowed to sell the meat, but they could use it for their own consumption. I'm sure they were allowed to give beef away, but they did.

TIPS ON COOKING BEEF

There are 2 methods of cooking beef: dry and moist heat. Dry heat is roasting and broiling. Moist heat includes braising and stewing. The more tender pieces can be cooked by dry heat.

TO ROAST, place meat in uncovered pan and cook with fat side up at 300° until tender. If you like the crustiness for gravy, you may sear it. No liquid is added.

TO BROIL steak, set the rack about 3 inches below the flame. If the steaks are 1 1/2 inches thick, place on hot rack and broil about 4 minutes. Then broil 3 to 4 minutes on the other side.

TO PAN BROIL, put beef in a heavy hot skillet. Let it brown on one side and then turn to brown the other side. Let fry in its own fat and keep pouring off the fat, or you'll have a fried piece of meat, instead of pan broiled.

TO BRAISE, use less tender cuts, cover and cook slowly. No basting is necessary, but there should be just enough liquid to keep plenty of steam for the meat. The liquid can be stock, sour cream, mushroom soup, etc. Never boil.

TO SEAR add very little fat to roaster. Place the beef tightly on the spot where you want it to stay. Press lightly to seal in the juices and don't move until brown. Treat the other side is the same manner. When brown, the beef is ready for the oven.

POT ROAST
(braised meat casserole)
circa 1910

Suitable for large lean pieces of beef (round or rump), shoulder of veal, mutton (whole or in portion), foul, liver or any meat that has a tough fiber and needs slow, gentle moist heat to soften it, and also the rich flavor given by slow heat.

Wipe, trim and fry out some of the fat in kettle (for veal use half salt pork and kidney suet). Brown sliced onions in fat, dredge meat with flour, brown it all over in the fat, add 1 cup of water, cover tightly. Cook slowly 4-6 hours or until very tender. Replenish with 1/2 cup of water, if needed. Always add small amounts of water at a time. Season and thicken for gravy.

BEST ROAST

5-7 pound rump roast. Rub the roast with suet and heat until it is very hot. Sear meat on all sides. Add about 1/4 - 1/2 cup of water and cover with lid tightly. Cook 300° for 35 minutes per pound. There will be plenty broth for rice or noodles. Good for sandwiches. You can add potatoes, carrots and whole onions around the roast. Try searing roast with kidney suet. It makes a world of difference in taste. Now you've got it made! Good for getting or keeping your man.

BROWN GRAVY FROM ROAST BEEF

3 Tbsp. fat
2 Tbsp. flour
3 Tbsp. cold water
1 3/4 cup hot water
Worchestershire sauce

Remove roast from pan, but leave 3 Tbsp. of fat in pan. Place over low heat and scrape down the crusty particles. Mix the flour and cold water to make a smooth paste. Strain the flour mixture into hot fat, stirring constantly. Add hot water and stir until smooth. Increase heat and let gravy boil for 5 minutes. Add salt and pepper and a few drops of Worchestershire sauce. If you want more, increase portions and add some beef bouillon cubes. Use milk for cream gravy, and it should be thicker than roast gravy.

BARBEQUED ROAST

4 lbs. boneless lean roast
2 Tbsp. vinegar
2 Tbsp. brown sugar
4 Tbsp. lemon juice
4 cups or 32 oz. bottle catsup
2 Tbsp. Worchestershire sauce
1 Tbsp. chili powder
1 1/2 cup water
1 large onion (chopped)
1/2 cup celery (chopped)

Place roast in roaster and cover with onions and celery. Mix remaining ingredients and pour over roast. Cover and bake 3 hours at 350°. Do not peek. Cool and slice. This recipe will also make a lot of sandwiches and will freeze well.

BROILED STEAK
circa 1910

Have your steak at least 1 1/2 inches thick, trim off the fat, leaving only a rim around the edge. Have the wire broiler well greased with suet and very hot. Lay the steak on a place exposed to a blaze that will quickly sear the surface without burning the fat. Then turn and sear the other side in the same manner. When this is done, turn again and broil about 5 minutes on the other side. Have a heated platter with a tablespoon of melted butter, lay the steak on this platter and season with salt and pepper. Pour a little melted butter over surface of the steak. Serve very hot. When properly broiled, the interior of the steak is pink and juicy.

FRIED MEAT
circa 1910

Small chops, cutlets of veal and portions of tripe may be covered with bread crumbs, dipped in beaten egg and dipped again in bread crumbs. Fry in deep hot fat. Reduce heat after the first plunge, so they will not be too brown when done, or cook them in a little of their own fat, in a spider (a long handle iron frying pan with attached legs for use over an open fire).

KITCHEN KAPERS: Try sprinkling poppy seed on cooked noodles.

STEAMED MEAT
circa 1910

Use bones and trimmings from roasts or the tough parts of steaks and chops, the legs, neck and wings of poultry, or use tough, cheap portions of any kind of fresh meat, first browning some of the lean in melted suet or fat of the meat with a sliced onion to give the flavor of roast meat. Use onions and turnips cut small with all meat; celery or sweet pepper with poultry; parsnips with pork; rice and tomato with veal. Remove the fat and bones. Add the vegetables, and 20 minutes before serving, add sliced potatoes, first scalding them to prevent their juice from giving the broth an unpleasant flavor. Thicken the water, season to taste.

If desired, add 10 minutes before serving, dumplings made with 1 pint flour, 1/2 level tsp. of salt and 1 rounded tsp. of baking powder. Moisten with milk to make a soft dough. Use no shortening if you wish them to be light. Eggs are not necessary. Drop the dough from a teaspoon into boiling stew, letting them rest on meat or potatoes, or toss dough on floured board, roll out and cut with small cutter. Keep covered tightly and cook just 10 minutes.

"Prove all things; hold fast that which is good."
1 Thessalonians 5:21

MEAT LOAF

1 lb. ground beef
1/2 cup evaporated milk
1/3 cup oats (not cooked)
1/4 cup chopped onions
1 tsp. salt
1/8 tsp. pepper

Mix the above ingredients and cook for 10 minutes.

Mix these ingredients:

1 cup tomato sauce
2 Tbsp. brown sugar
1 Tbsp. vinegar
1 tsp. Worchestershire sauce
1/4 tsp. dry mustard
1/2 tsp. chili pepper
1/2 tsp. salt

Stir 1/2 of the above mixture into the meat mixture. Place in loaf pan and pour rest of sauce over the meat mixture. Bake at 350° for 50 minutes.

MRS. MILLS' CORNED BEEF HASH
85 yr. old recipe

To 1 pint of chopped meat, add 1 1/2 pints of chopped, cooked potatoes. Melt 1/3 cup of lard or salt pork drippings in a skillet and add 2 Tbsp. of minced onions. Mix the hash thoroughly with the fat and season well, adding just enough water to moisten well (about 1/2 cup). Cover tightly and cook slowly for 1/2 hour, or until brown crust has formed on bottom. Loosen carefully from the pan and turn out on a hot platter.

MRS. MILLS' SWISS STEAK

1 1/2 lbs. of round steak
1/4 cup of flour
1 tsp. of salt
1/2 tsp. of pepper
3 Tbsp. of lard
1 can (1 lb.) of tomatoes
1 large onion (sliced)
1 green pepper (sliced)
1 stalk of celery (sliced)

Cut meat into serving pieces, trim off excess fat. Combine flour, salt and pepper. Pound flour into both sides of meat with edge of saucer. Heat oil in skillet. Add meat and brown slowly on both sides. Add all remaining ingredients. Heat until liquid is boiling. Then reduce to simmer, cover and simmer 1 1/2 hours or until meat is tender.

MARINATED BEEF BRISKET
Myrtle Truitt

4-5 lbs. brisket
Lowrey's seasoning salt
Garlic salt
Celery salt
Meat tenderizer
4 Tbsp. Worchestershire sauce
1/2 bottle liquid smoke (4 oz. size)

Trim off all fat, rub both sides with seasoned salt, tenderizer, garlic and celery salt. Put in pan or baking dish. Add Worchestershire sauce and liquid smoke. Cover and store in refrigerator for 24 hours. Bake uncovered or wrapped in foil at 225° for about 5 hours.

SALISBURY STEAK

1 lb. ground beef
1/2 cup quick cooking oats (uncooked)
2 Tbsp. water
1/2 tsp. dried onion (add more to taste,
      if desired)
1/2 tsp. salt
1 egg (beaten)
2 Tbsp. catsup
2 Tbsp. Worchestershire sauce
1/4 tsp. pepper
1 can cream mushroom soup
1 soup can of water

Combine beef, egg, oats, catsup, water, Worchestershire sauce, onions, salt and pepper. Form into patties and pat lightly in flour. Brown patties in large frying pan in butter. Pour off grease and combine soup and water. Pour over patties. Simmer for 45 minutes. Makes 5-6 steaks.

CREOLE MEAT SAUCE

1/2 lb. ground beef
3 Tbsp. fat
1/2 green pepper (chopped)
1/2 medium onion (chopped)
1/2 cup celery (chopped)
2 Tbsp. flour
1/2 tsp. chili powder
1/2 tsp. salt
1 no. 2 can tomatoes (don't drain)

Brown the beef in 3 Tbsp. of fat. Add pepper, onion, celery and cook until tender. Add tomatoes to make a sauce. Mix in heavy skillet with salt and chili powder. Add water, if needed. Cook slowly, 10-15 minutes. Serve over cooked rice or noodles.

MIKE ALLEN'S SOUTH OF THE RED RIVER "RED" CHILI

1/8 lb. chopped suet (finely chopped)
3 lbs. round steak (coarsely cubed)
6 Tbsp. chili powder
1 Tbsp. oregano
1 Tbsp. cumin seed
1 tsp. salt
1/2 to 1 Tbsp. cayenne
1 large clove garlic (minced)
1 Tbsp. Tabasco sauce (if you dare)
1 1/2 qts. water. Add more if needed.
1/2 cup corn meal
paprika
1 can tomato sauce

Saute` the suet, add more steak and the rest of the ingredients with water. Add more water if needed. Start on medium heat and turn to simmer for about 45 minutes. Add gradually 1/2 corn meal and stir until mixed well. Add paprika and tomato sauce for color and simmer for 30 minutes.

SPANISH RICE

Saute` 1 lb. ground beef in a small amount of oil. Add 1 cup of diced onions and chopped peppers. Diced celery would be good too. Use a heavy skillet. Add 1 can of tomato sauce and 2 cans of water. Add 3/4 cup of rice, and simmer until rice is done. Add chili powder to taste.

MEXICAN BEEF
circa 1907

The Mexicans have a dish known as Chili Con Carne (meat with chili pepper), the ingredients for which, one would doubtless have difficulty in obtaining, except in the Southwestern U.S. However, a good substitute for it may be made with the foods available in all parts of the country.

The Mexican recipe is as follows: remove the seeds from 2 chili peppers, soak the pods in a pint of warm water until they are soft. Scrape the pulp from the skin and add water. Cut 2 pounds of beef into small pieces and brown in butter or drippings. Add a clove of garlic and the chili water. Cook until the meat is tender, renewing the water if necessary. Thicken the sauce with flour. Serve with Mexican beans either mixed with the meat or use as a border.

In absence of the chili peppers, water and cayenne pepper may be used, and onions may be substituted for garlic. For the Mexican beans, red kidney beans either fresh or canned make a good substitute. If canned beans are used they should be drained and heated in a little savory fat or butter. The liquid could be added to the meat while it is cooking. If dried beans are used, the should be soaked until soft then cooked in water until tender and rather dry. A little butter (or drippings) and salt may be used for seasoning or gravy, and white or dried lima beans may be used in a similar way.

BILL'S NINE ONE ONE SALSA
Bill Pingley

2 cans (no. 2) whole peeled tomatoes
    (chopped)
1 medium onion (diced)
1/2 clove of garlic (minced)
1/2 tsp. of salt (optional)
2 medium jalapeno peppers

Coarsely chop 2 cans of whole peeled tomatoes. Drain the tomatoes and reserve 1/2 of the liquid and place in mixing bowl. Boil the jalapeno peppers in water until you can pull out the stem easily and then dice the peppers and place in mixing bowl. Add the rest of the ingredients. For a milder version of this recipe, throw out the jalapeno pepper seeds.

MARIE MILLS' STUFFED GREEN PEPPERS

1 lb. ground beef
6 large green peppers
1 large onion (minced)
1 clove of garlic (minced)
3 Tbsp. margarine (melted)
3 tomatoes (peeled and chopped)
1 Tbsp. Worchestershire sauce
1/2 tsp. salt
1/4 tsp. pepper
1 cup cooked rice
1/2 cup breadcrumbs (butter)

Cut off tops of green peppers. Cover in boiling water, cook for 5 minutes and drain. Cook beef, onion and garlic in margarine, stirring to crumble meat. Add tomatoes. Simmer 10 minutes. Add the rest of the ingredients, except breadcrumbs. Mix. Stuff peppers with beef mixture, place in shallow baking dish. Top with breadcrumbs. Bake at 350° for 25 minutes. Serves 6.

"SO GOOD" BEEF STROGANOFF

1 lb. sirloin steak (cut in 2 1/2" strips)
1/2 cup onion (minced)
1 clove garlic (minced)
2 Tbsp. shortening
1/2 tsp. salt
1/8 tsp. pepper
1 can (3 oz.) mushrooms (sliced)
1 cup beef bouillon
1/2 cup sour cream
2 Tbsp. catsup

Cook wide noodles that have been drained and rinsed in hot water. Saute` garlic and onions in hot shortening. Remove from skillet. Dredge beef in combined flour, salt and pepper. Brown over low heat. Return onion and garlic to skillet, add catsup and 1 cup of bouillon. Cover tightly and simmer for 1 hour or until meat is tender. Stir occasionally. If mixture becomes too thick, add more bouillon. Uncover and add quickly the sour cream and heat thoroughly. Serve over hot noodles sprinkled with poppy seeds.

SYLVIA'S MOCK STEAK CASSEROLE
Sylvia Worcester

2 lbs. ground beef
2 eggs (raw)
1 cup <u>each</u> of finely grated carrots,
      onion and potato
2 cans of any cream soup (cream of
      chicken, celery, broccoli, onion,
      mushroom, or cheese - 10 3/4
      oz.)
2 empty soup cans of milk

Mix ground beef, eggs, carrots, onion and potato in a large bowl. Form mixture into medium sized patties. Fry in vegetable oil until done. Salt and pepper to taste. Drain patties well on paper towels. This recipe makes 2 casseroles -- one to eat now and one to freeze for later. Layer meat patties into 2 dishes (1 1/2 to 2 quarts each). Spread 1 can of your favorite cream soup on top layer of patties in each dish. Then pour 1 empty soup can full of milk over each. Cover. Bake at 350° for approximately 1 hour, or until soup and milk make gravy.

BARBEQUE SAUCE

6 cups tomato juice
6 tsp. Worchestershire sauce
6 Tbsp. soy sauce
2-4 packages artificial sweetener

Simmer all ingredients until thickens for about 20 minutes. Good for marinating roasts. Also good on fish and chicken.

VENISON ROAST

Wash the meat in salt water to remove blood. Salt and pepper to taste. Poke deep holes in the roast with the point of a very sharp knife. Fasten 2-4 strips of salt pork around the roast with toothpicks. The bacon fat will penetrate the roast through the holes.

Put the meat in a roasting pan. Add about 1 cup of water for a 4 to 5 lb. roast. Place in 325° oven for 1 hour, turning a time or two. Now cover and cook same temperature for 2 hours. You can make gravy thicken from juices, but the natural juices seem to be better. Since venison tallows quickly, serve on heated platter.

"A man that hath friends must show himself friendly; and there is a friend that sticketh closer than a brother."
Proverbs 18:24

WISDOM

When the azure blue of the morning
Turns gold at the set of the sun,
And the black velvet night draws around us,
And I think of the things I have done;

Can I honestly say I'm a giver
Of the things that bring gladness and cheer?
Did I help some old soldier of Jesus
As the twilight if life draweth near?

Did I take time to listen with interest
To the counsel of one who has earned
By the passage of time and much trouble,
The right to convey what he's learned?

Did I see myself in the mirror
Of the vision he paints so sublime;
And did I learn from the listening...this lesson,
That life's greatest teacher is time?

Did I pause in the midst of life's hurry
To give just a little of me
To one who soon will be sailing
His soul on eternity's sea?

I ask...for I think I have seen it,
Why God allows saints to grow old,
The counsel...the wisdom they offer
Can't be purchased with silver and gold.

So listen to one who has lived it,
And has come through the storm and the strife,
His words, bearing echoes of heaven,
Bespeak of eternal life!

Marion E. Lobaugh
Minister of Elm & Hudson Church of Christ
Altus, Oklahoma

FISH

On Saturday mornings in the summertime, my mother would tell us if we would hurry up and get a particular job done we could go fishing later in the afternoon. Our farm had bottom land, and the creek ran at the edge. The creek only had small fish, and our catch was small. I believe we caught mainly catfish. Our fishing poles were cut from mesquite limbs, and the cork was really cork from a bottle.

The most fun we had fishing was swimming. We didn't have swim suits, but we used our petti-skirts and took clean clothes to wear back to the house. We took soap and wash rags. The lye soap was handy; it floated. This fun outing also served as our Saturday night bath. I remember how refreshing it was.

FRIED CATFISH

catfish
1 cup milk
2 green peppers (chopped)
6 sour pickles (chopped)
1 egg (beaten)
crumbs
1 Tbsp. flour
salt and pepper to taste

Cut fish into small servings. Season fish with salt and pepper. Dip in crumbs and brush with egg. Dip in crumbs again. Fry in deep shortening until browned. Drain on brown paper. Dip 1 1/2 Tbsp. of hot shortening from kettle into a saucepan. Blend in flour and stir in milk gradually. Cook, stirring constantly until smooth and thickened. Cool. Stir in green pepper and pickles. Serve over fish.

CATFISH AND GEORGIA BOG GRAVY

3 lbs. catfish (dressed)
cornmeal
3 cups potatoes (diced)
1 cup onions (diced)
1 can (no. 2) tomatoes
1 can tomato juice
2 Tbsp. salt
1 tsp. pepper

Sprinkle 1 1/2 Tbsp. salt over fish and coat in 1 cup cornmeal. Fry in deep fat until golden brown and drain on paper towels. Drain all but 1/2 cup fat from pan and stir in 1 Tbsp. cornmeal. Add potatoes and onions; cover. Cook until potatoes are tender. Stir in tomatoes, tomato juice, remaining salt and pepper. Cook, stirring until thickened.

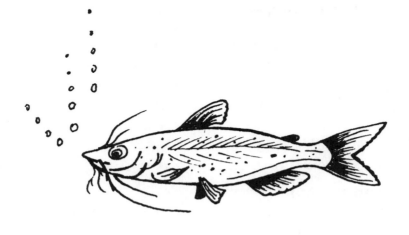

We had a tank (man-made pond), where we watered our cows and horses. Marie and I were allowed to crawfish in the tank without supervision, because the water was shallow. All we had to do to catch them was tie a piece of bacon to a twine line attached to a mesquite pole. We could pull them out about as fast as we could bait the line. Sometimes, we would bait a bent pin with salt pork.

One time when Marie and I were crawfishing, we had a visit from my father's cousin and his children. It was quite a surprise, since they lived quite a distance away. They joined us in crawfishing, and in "nothing flat" we had a tubful of crawfish that we cleaned and fried for a big meal. This is the only time I remember eating crawfish, but I understand they are a delicacy in some areas.

QUICK AND EASY FILLETS OF SOLE

1 1/2 lbs. sole
2 egg whites (stiffly beaten)
1/4 cup almonds (chopped)
1 small onion (peeled and minced)
2 Tbsp. lemon juice
1 Tbsp. mayonnaise
salt and pepper to taste

Brush fillets with lemon juice and broil 5 minutes. Combine remaining ingredients and spread over fillets. Brown under broiler. Serves 4.

KITCHEN KAPERS: To chop fresh parsley, wash and put into narrow jelly glass and chop with kitchen scissors until divided.

SEAFOOD CASSEROLE

3 hard cooked eggs
1 can (5 oz.) shrimp (cut)
1 can (7 oz.) tuna (drained)
1 can (2 oz.) mushrooms
1 can (6 1/2 oz.) crabmeat
2 cups medium cream sauce
1/4 lb. cheddar cheese (grated)
1 cup bread crumbs
1/4 lb. butter (melted)

Put layers of eggs, shrimp, tuna, crabmeat and mushrooms in a buttered casserole, pouring part of cream sauce over each layer. Sprinkle top with cheese and the buttered bread crumbs. Bake at 350° for 45 minutes.

TUNA STRAW CASSEROLE

1 can tuna (7 or 9 1/4 oz.) drained
1 can cream of mushroom soup
1 can (6 oz.) evaporated milk
1 can (3 oz.) broiled sliced mushrooms
    (drained)
1/4 cup chopped pimento
1 can (4 oz.) shoestring potatoes

Reserve 1 cup shoestring potatoes for top. Combine the remaining ingredients and pour into 1 1/2 quart casserole dish. Arrange reserved potatoes on top. Cook at 350° for 20 to 25 minutes or until thoroughly heated.

TUNA WITH RICE

1 cup tuna or small can
1 cup rice (cooked)
1 egg (beaten)
1 cup thin white sauce
1 Tbsp. butter
1 tsp. salt

Cook rice and add butter and salt. Mix lightly. Line oiled dish with rice and pour tuna over this and cover with white sauce to which egg has been added. Bake at 375° for 30 minutes.

WHITE SAUCE

1 cup milk (cold)
2 Tbsp. flour
2 Tbsp. butter or margarine
1/4 tsp. salt
1/8 tsp. pepper

Mix ingredients in a saucepan. Heat to boiling over medium heat, stirring constantly. Boil for 1 minute.

SHAKE AND BAKE MIXTURE
for fish and chicken

4 cups corn flakes
1 envelope (6 oz.) dry zesty Italian
        dressing mix (Knorr brand)
2 Tbsp. Parmesan cheese
2 Tbsp. parsley flakes

Crush corn flakes in food processor or blender until fine crumbs. Add Parmesan cheese and parsley flakes. Store in plastic storage bag until ready to use.

TUNA ALMONDINE
Olevia Robinson

2 1/2 Tbsp. flour
2 1/2 cups milk
2 1/2 Tbsp. butter
14 cup American cheese (chunks)
2 cans tuna
2 Tbsp. toasted almonds
1/4 cup American cheese (grated)

Mix 2 1/2 Tbsp. flour, 2 1/2 cups of milk and 2 1/2 Tbsp. of butter in saucepan. Heat to boiling point for 1 minute, stirring constantly. When thick add 1/2 cup of American cheese.

Cook 8 oz. medium width egg noodles. Rinse in hot water and drain. Add noodles to sauce with 1/4 cup of pimentos and 1/4 cup of toasted almonds.

Drain oil from 2 cans of tuna, break up with a fork and fold into sauce mixture. Pour into 2 quart casserole dish. Sprinkle with 1/4 cup of grated cheese and 2 Tbsp. of toasted almonds. Bake at 375° for about 20 minutes and the lower heat to 325° for 15 minutes more.

SALMON CROQUETTES

1 large can red or pink salmon
2 eggs (lightly beaten)
1 cup mashed potatoes
salt and pepper to taste
1 Tbsp. lemon juice
1/4 tsp. shortening

Drain salmon and remove skin and bones. Discard skin, mash salmon fine, crush bones and add to salmon. Stir in eggs and salmon with juice and potatoes, blending well. Add seasoning and lemon juice, mix thoroughly. Divide in 1/2 cup portions and shape into cones. Heat shortening in heavy skillet. Lay in patties. Start on flat side, then roll to brown the cone. Brown in slow medium heat. Serve with catsup or tartar sauce.

SALMON LOAF
Cleo Campbell

1 large can red or pink salmon
2/3 cup evaporated milk
2 cups soft bread crumbs
1 egg (beaten)
1 Tbsp. parsley (minced)
2 Tbsp. onion (minced)
1/2 tsp. salt
1/4 tsp. poultry seasoning
1/4 tsp. Tabasco sauce

Remove skin and bones from salmon and do not drain. Combine the salmon and liquid with evaporated milk and bread crumbs in a bowl. Mix with a fork until well blended. Add beaten egg, parsley, onion, salt, poultry seasoning and Tabasco sauce. Mix well. Place in a greased loaf pan 9 x 4 x 3 inches and bake at 375° for 40 minutes. Serves 4.

SCALLOPED OYSTERS
circa 1910

Crush and roll several handfuls of Boston or other breakable crackers. Put a layer in the bottom of a buttered pudding dish. Wet this with a mixture of the oyster liquid and milk, slightly warmed. Next, have a layer of oysters. Sprinkle with salt and pepper and dot with butter. Then add another layer of moistened crumbs and so on until the dish is full. Let the top layer be of crumbs, thicker than the rest and beat an egg into the milk you pour over them. Dot with butter. Cover the dish, set in oven, bake half an hour. If the dish be large, remove the cover and brown by setting it upon the upper grating of the oven, or by holding a hot shovel over it.

SCALLOPED SCALLOPS

1 1/2 lbs. scallops
1/4 cup butter
4 cups soft bread crumbs
1 tsp. onions (finely minced)
1 tsp. parsley (finely minced)
1 tsp. chives (minced)
1 Tbsp. lemon juice
1 1/4 tsp. salt

Melt butter in deep skillet. Add bread crumbs, onions, parsley, chives, lemon juice and salt. Toss together while cooking. Cook for 5 minutes. In a well buttered casserole dish, arrange a layer of the bread crumb mixture and scallops, using bread crumbs as top layer. If scallops are large, cut in quarters. Bake in hot oven (400°) for about 20 minutes until golden brown. Serve hot from casserole dish. Serves 6.

TARTAR SAUCE

For egg and fish salads, fried fish, oysters, scallops, etc. To 1 cup mayonnaise add: 2 Tbsp. sweet pickles (ground), 1 Tbsp. capers (ground), 1 Tbsp. olives (ground), and 1 Tbsp. chives (ground). Mix.

FRUITS
AND
VEGETABLES

We knew nothing about nutrition, let alone calories. I'm sure one of the reasons our mothers and grandmothers unscientific method of filling up her family was nutritionally successful, most cases, was because we had bigger families and bigger appetites. Everyone worked harder than most of us do today. A hundred years ago, 80% of our population lived on farms. In those days there were few of the labor saving devices that we take for granted in the days of electricity and power-driven motors. Everybody worked hard and had increased appetites. We lived in colder, draftier houses and needed more food to keep us warm and for energy. It was the amount we ate that furnished sufficient nutrients for good health. The food was different and we ate more which automatically gave us more of these necessary nutrients. We had far less variety of food than we enjoy today. Since we lived on farms, the food was fresh from the fields, orchards and gardens with most of the nutrients intact. The only oranges we had were stuffed in Christmas stockings. Now you can buy oranges and fruit juices anytime. We really lived off the land.

There were root cellars and pits for cabbage, carrots, turnips and apples that kept them until spring. Storm cellars stored everything we could can. Some fruits, covered with cheesecloth to keep the flies off, were dried very successfully on top of the smokehouse. Corn, beans and peas were also dried.

Potatoes were dug with a turning plow and left in the field to dry for a few hours. We stored our potatoes under the house. We raked them out with a hoe or broomstick when needed. When we could no longer reach them, Marie or I had to crawl under the house to get them. Sometimes we would encounter a snake, but we always gave him "wagon room." This food would tide is over until the spring greens came in.

These wild greens included lambsquarter, polk salad and dandelions. Town folks would think the greens were weeds, but they did not know what they were missing. They were so good seasoned with salt pork. We took the large stems from the polk salad, sliced them and fried them with meal batter. We called it "mock" okra. Hard cooked eggs were served with the greens.

TURNIP GREENS WITH POT LIQUOR DUMPLINGS

2 lbs. fresh young turnip greens
1/4 lb. salt pork
water

GREENS

Enough water to have 3-4 cups liquid when done (pot liquor). Clean and wash greens. Combine salt pork and water, then add greens. Cover and cook greens until tender. Put greens in bowl and cover to keep warm.

DUMPLINGS

1 cup corn meal
1/2 tsp. salt
2/3 cup boiling water
Pot liquor

Put cornmeal and salt in bowl to mix. Stir boiling water into cornmeal mixture and blend well. Use a heaping Tbsp. for each portion, shape into balls and place into pot liquor from the greens. Simmer slowly, until dumplings are done, for 20 to 30 minutes. Remove from heat and let stand for 10 minutes. They are now ready to serve, and you don't have to make cornbread. Serve with sliced onions.

GREEN SPINACH
circa 1900

Pick over and look for insects, trim and wash five times in water. Drain and put into kettle with water that drips from them. Cook slowly at first until juice is drawn out, then cook quickly until tender. Drain and rinse if you dislike the strong flavor. Chop, reheat and season with butter, salt and pepper. Add cream if you like or serve with lemon or vinegar. If for a main course, garnish with hard boiled eggs, or serve cold for salad.

In the old days, salt pork and butter were used together for seasoning.

SWEET AND SOUR CABBAGE
Different and Delicious

4 cups shredded cabbage
salt and pepper to taste
a dash of celery seed
1 small onion (chopped)
3 slices bacon
3 Tbsp. vinegar
3 Tbsp. sugar

Cook cabbage in small amount of boiling water until tender for not more than 10 minutes. Drain and add salt, pepper, celery seed and onion. Fry bacon until crisp and save drippings. Mince the bacon and add to cabbage. Stir vinegar and sugar into hot drippings. Let boil up once. Pour over cabbage mixture and serve immediately. Pass the hot cornbread with plenty of butter.

63

LYE HOMINY
circa 1890

Put scant Tbsp. of lye in heavy iron kettle (never aluminum). Cautiously, add 1 gallon of boiling water. When lye hits the water, it will boil up. If lye touches the skin, it will cause a bad burn. Add 2 quarts of dry shelled corn (preferably white). Stir, let stand overnight. Next morning, place over fire and heat to boiling. Stir with stainless or wooden spoon. Simmer 20 minutes until husks on cob are loosened. Drain off lye water and rinse with cold water about 3 times. Turn corn into an enamelware colander and place under running water for 15 minutes. Lift corn with spoon to expose the hominy to the rinsing water. This rinsing should be done until the husks are gone. Put back into same kettle that has been scrubbed clean. Cover well with water. Simmer about 3 hours. Add more water, if needed. Cover with liquid. Put in jars and seal with new lids.

SUCCOTASH

2 cups fresh green or lima beans
2 cups fresh corn
1 cup milk
2 Tbsp. butter

Cook corn and beans until done. Cook onions in small amount of water. Add onions to the rest of ingredients and simmer for about 10 minutes.

My sister and I helped my mother fry corn in this manner.

FRIED CORN

Select 12 ears of corn at the perfect stage. Husk the corn and remove silk by brushing back and forth with a soft brush or cloth. Cut from the cob with a very sharp knife. Cut only half the depth of the kernel. Use the back of the knife to scrape out the remaining pulp and juice. Scrape downward only enough for 5 cups of corn. Heat 1/2 cup of butter, sizzling hot in heavy skillet. Add corn and enough water to give consistency of thin gravy. Season with salt and pepper, stirring constantly. Cook 5 minutes. Reduce heat to simmering. Cover tightly and cook about 20 minutes longer. The corn will be thick. Serve hot. Very good with fried chicken.

Squash came in early and was easy to grow.

FRIED SQUASH

4 medium squash
cornmeal
1 medium onion (diced with tops)
enough lard to fry

Slice squash into 1/2 inch pieces. Coat well with cornmeal. Fry squash and onions in lard until golden brown.

My mother made green tomato pie before the ripe tomatoes were in season. This pie gave my mother another dish to feed the family.

GREEN TOMATO PIE

6 medium size green tomatoes
2 Tbsp. water
1/2 lemon (sliced)
4 Tbsp. flour
1 cup sugar
1/8 tsp. salt
1/4 tsp. cinnamon
2 Tbsp. butter

Wash tomatoes, remove blossom end and cut into thin slices. Cook tomatoes, water and lemon until nearly tender. Let cool and add the flour which has been mixed with sugar and salt. Cook until thickened. Stir in butter and cinnamon. Pour in partially baked pie shell. For the top crust, cut a circle smaller than the bottom crust. No need to prick shell. It will have steam escape. Cook about 30 minutes.

BAKED SQUASH AND SAUSAGE

3 acorn squash (we used more, because
        we needed "left-overs" for supper)
about 1 lb. of bulk sausage

Cut squash into halves, arrange squash, cut side down, in shallow greased baking pan. Bake in moderate oven for 20 minutes. Shape sausage into 6 small patties and brown slightly in skillet. Turn squash and sprinkle with salt and pepper. Put sausage in each squash half. Bake for about 20 minutes or until sausage is done and squash is tender.

DILLED ACORN SQUASH

4 cups acorn squash (peeled and
    cubed)
salt
2 Tbsp. green onions (sliced with tops)
1 Tbsp. butter
1/2 cup sour cream
2 Tbsp. milk
a dash of pepper
1/2 tsp. dill seed

Cook squash in boiling salted (very little) water for about 10 minutes, or until tender. Drain well. Keep warm and put on back of stove. Cook green onions in butter until tender, blend in sour cream, milk, salt and pepper to taste. Bring just to a boil. Arrange squash on platter. Top with sour cream mixture and sprinkle with dill seed.

SAUCE FOR NEW POTATOES
fit for a king

Boil the amount of potatoes desired until tender. Make plenty of white sauce to which you have added chopped parsley or flakes. Salt and pepper to taste. Make sauce with plenty of cream and butter. Pour over potatoes and simmer for a few minutes.

KITCHEN KAPERS: Add caraway seeds or dry parsley to new potatoes with white sauce.

FRIED IRISH POTATOES

Cut peeled Irish potatoes in 1/4 inch pieces. Roll in cornmeal to coat and season to taste with salt and pepper. Fry in 1/4 cup lard until crisp. You may have to add more lard. Serve with salt pork and gravy.

POTATO CASSEROLE
Nada Jean Thomas

8 potatoes (cook, cool, and dice)
1 1/2 cups cheese (shredded)
2 cans cream of chicken soup
1 pint sour cream
1/4 to 1/2 cup onions (chopped)
1/4 cup margarine (melted)
cornflakes

Mix ingredients and put in large flat dish. Mix 1 cup of crushed cornflakes with 2 Tbsp. of margarine and scatter on top, cover, refrigerate overnight. Bake at 350° for 35 - 40 minutes, uncovered.

POOR MAN'S OYSTERS
in memory of Visa Hayes

6 medium tomatoes (sliced)
1 medium onion (chopped fine)
1/4 tsp. salt
1/4 tsp. sugar
1/2 cup cornmeal
1/4 cup flour
pepper to taste
1/3 cup lard

Heat lard in skillet and saute` onions in the skillet. Put tomato slices in the mixed cornmeal and flour. Cook in hot lard for 2 minutes on each side or until brown.

MRS. MILLS' OKRA GUMBO
(SOUTHERN STYLE)

this recipe is from a 1910 newspaper that
Mrs. Mills pasted in a notebook

1 chicken
2 lbs. beef
1 large onion
1/2 pod of red pepper with seeds
      removed
2 pints of okra or about 50 pods
2 slices of ham
6 tomatoes
1 bay leaf
1 sprig of thyme or parsley
1 Tbsp. each of lard and butter
salt and cayenne pepper to taste

Clean and cut up the chicken, cube the beef, cut the ham in small squares or dice, and chop the onions, parsley and thyme. Skin tomatoes and chop fine, saving the juice. Wash and stem the okra and slice into thin layers of 1/2 inch. Put lard and butter into a soup kettle, when hot, add the chicken and ham. Cover closely and let simmer for 10 minutes. Then add the tomatoes, parsley, thyme and chopped onions, stirring constantly to keep from sticking. Add the okra and when well browned, add the juice from tomato. The okra is very delicate and is liable to scorch if not attended often. When well fried and brown, add about 3 quarts of boiling water and set on back of stove to simmer for 1 hour or more. Serve hot with boiled rice.

HARVARD BEETS
an old recipe

6 beets or more as desired (diced)
2/3 cups sugar
2 Tbsp. cornstarch or flour (it takes
        more flour)
1/2 cup vinegar
1/2 tsp. salt
1/4 cup butter

Scrub beets well, remove beet tops, leaving roots and 1 inch stem. Cook in boiling water for 50 to 60 minutes. Rub skins off beets. Drain beets, save 1/2 cup liquid. Mix sugar and cornstarch in saucepan. Blend in reserved hot liquid, vinegar and salt. Bring to a boil, stirring constantly. Move to back of stove and simmer for 2 minutes. Add beets and simmer for 15 minutes longer. Stir in butter just before serving.

FRIED TURNIPS
an old recipe

turnips
salt
flour
1 egg (beaten)
bread crumbs (finely ground)
lard

Peel turnips and cut into 1/2 inch slices. Cook into boiling salted water until just tender. Drain and cool. Combine egg with 1 Tbsp. water, dip slices in flour, then in egg mixture and then dip in bread crumbs again. Fry turnips in small amount of hot lard in skillet until brown on both sides.

SCRATCH BAKED BEANS
This prize-winning recipe was given to me by Joy Bellizzi

2 lbs. Navy beans
salt and pepper to taste
1/2 lb. pork side meat (fresh and sliced)
1 small onion (minced)
1 can cream of tomato soup
1 soup can of water
1 cup brown sugar
1/4 cup molasses
1 tsp. dry mustard.
2 Tbsp. vinegar

Pick and wash beans. Soak overnight in enough water to cover 3 inches above level of beans. Drain and cover with more water and cook very slowly until beans are barely tender. Drain well and add salt and pepper to taste. Fry the pork (do not brown) while the beans are cooling. Remove slices and put aside. Add onions to fat and cook slowly. Add other ingredients and let simmer for a few minutes. Put in beans, let stand overnight to blend flavor and give a better flavor. Put beans in heavy pot (Dutch oven is good). Bake at 300° for 3 hours. You'll need to stir a time or two. Place pork slices on top to brown. Bake about 30 minutes longer, or until pork is brown.

"A man's gift maketh room for him, and bringeth him before great men."
Proverbs 18:16

HERBED TOMATOES

6 ripe tomatoes
2/3 cup vinegar
1/4 cup snipped parsley or flakes
1/4 cup sliced green onions (blades and
       all)
1 tsp. salt
1/4 tsp. pepper
1/2 tsp. thyme
1 clove of garlic (minced)
2/3 cup salad oil

Peel tomatoes; place in bowl. Combine remaining ingredients in a jar and cover. Shake well and pour over tomatoes. Chill and cover, overnight. Spoon dressing over tomatoes occasionally.

Scalloped tomatoes were something my mother could make during season or from canned tomatoes.

SCALLOPED TOMATOES

4 large tomatoes (sliced)
2 Tbsp. butter
1/4 cup onions (chopped)
4 day old biscuits (cubed)
1 tsp. salt
1 tsp. sugar
1 tsp. pepper

Cook until tomatoes are tender. Add rest of ingredients except for bread crumbs. Cook down until rather low, if you want it thick, or leave it thin enough to eat with a spoon. Add crumbs last and simmer until crumbs are heated through.

If I wanted to make a hit with my husband, Marvin, and his brothers, all I had to do was make their mother's noodles. She used 1 can of tomatoes and lots of cream, added last. Sometimes, she used the noodles for soup and added more tomatoes, desired seasoning, chili powder, celery salt, garlic, salt, cayenne pepper and onions.

LOU ALLEN'S EGG NOODLES WITH TOMATOES
my mother-in-law's 100 year old recipe

Beat 1 egg slightly, add 1/2 tsp. salt. Gradually add 1 cup of flour or enough to make a stiff dough. Let stand a few minutes. Knead 5 minutes on a "dough board" and roll out paper thin. Cover with a towel and let dry for 20 minutes. Roll like a jelly roll and cut into strips of the desired width. Unroll and boil about 15 minutes in beef stock. My mother-in-law cooked with canned tomatoes with butter and cream added. Pepper may be added. If you need more noodles, add 1/2 egg shell of water, 1 level Tbsp. of shortening and 1/2 tsp. baking powder and enough flour to make a stiff dough. Easy to make and so good!

CANNED SAUERKRAUT
my mother's recipe

Wash and cut cabbage fine and pack tightly in fruit jars. Pour water over them until the cabbage is covered, then put on top of each jar 1 Tbsp. of salt. Put on lids, leaving them quite loose until the kraut has ceased to ferment. It will only take a few days, then it's time to seal the jars and put in a cool place.

MARIE MILLS' HERB RICE

1/4 stick margarine
1 medium onion (chopped)
1 cup long grain rice
2 chicken or beef bouillon cubes
3 1/2 to 4 cups water
salt to taste
3/4 tsp. Fines herbs (Spice Island)

Saute' onion and rice in margarine until brown. Add water, bouillon, Fines herbs. Cook covered slowly until rice is tender.

We always used 1/2 gallon jars to can fresh green beans, black-eyed peas, tomatoes and kraut. The canned fruits were peaches, blackberries, wild plums and wild green grapes. We used 1/2 gallon jars so we could have enough for dinner and supper. Nobody told us we didn't like left-overs.

The plums and grapes grew wild in the creek bottom. We gathered the green grapes before the seeds were matured. They tasted like gooseberries. We had fun swinging on the grapevines and never broke an arm or a leg, probably because we drank milk 3 times a day. We didn't get the idea of swinging from vines from Tarzan: he got it from us.

Do you know what Chickasaw plums are? They are the truly native plum of the Southern and Southwestern United States brought to Oklahoma by the Indians over two hundred years ago. They grow wild everywhere: along the highways, creek bottoms and woods. Some folks call them sand hill plums or wild plums. Whatever you call them, they make the best jelly or cobblers.

Aunt Lela was my mother's sister, the oldest of 8 children. Her mother died when she was 16 years old, and she reared the family with youngest one being 5 months old. She was a great cook and had to be a great manager to rear 8 children in those days.

Aunt Lela had a wonderful sense of humor. Her family was on a trip in the car when it died on the road and would not start. The driver wanted everyone out to push. Aunt Lela stated, "I'll get out, but I'm not going to push. These things weren't made to push."

Aunt Lela gave this recipe to my mother, and she passed it down to me.

AUNT LELA'S PLUM COBBLER

1/2 gallon canned plums
2 pints water
sugar to taste (according to the tartness
        of fruit)
4 Tbsp. butter

Put into a deep pan and let it come to a rolling boil.

The crust is made from a rich biscuit dough.

DOUGH

2 cups flour
a scant 1/2 cup lard
2 tsp. baking soda
1/4 tsp. salt
1/4 tsp. baking soda
buttermilk

Mix the 5 ingredients with enough buttermilk to handle easily. Turn on a floured board and knead slightly. Put crust in two balls. Roll out the first ball, as for making rolled dumplings. Put dumplings into the boiling fruit. Roll out the balance for top crust. Extend top crust about 1 inch above the fruit.

Before putting crust on top, prick the crust for air vents, close to center. If the vents are close to the center, the juice will not be lost.

Before putting in a moderately hot oven, dot with butter and sprinkle with a handful of sugar. Usually when the fruit starts to bubble, it's done. Serve warm with whipped cream.

Any fruit can be substituted in this recipe.

My grandmother doubled this recipe to make vinegar cobbler. We made this pie before the wild grapes and plums were in season, since vinegar was available.

VINEGAR PIE

2 cups boiling water
1/4 cup vinegar
1 cup sugar
3 Tbsp. flour
3 eggs
1 tsp. lemon flavoring
1/3 tsp. salt
3 Tbsp. sugar

Beat egg yolks until thick. Add 1 cup sugar, flour and salt. Mix thoroughly. Add boiling water slowly, stirring constantly. Add vinegar. Cook over hot water until thick and smooth. Add salt and flavoring. Pour into baked pastry shell. Cover with meringue made of egg whites and 3 Tbsp. of sugar. Bake in slow oven at 325° for 20 minutes.

FRIED GREEN APPLES

Core and slice enough green tart apples to fill a large skillet. Add apples to 2 or 3 Tbsp. of hot bacon grease. Cover and steam 10 minutes, then sprinkle the apples with 1 tsp. salt, 1/2 to 1 cup granulated sugar, 1/2 to 1 cup brown sugar, and Tbsp. lemon juice. Cover and cook, slowly stirring to prevent sticking. Add water if needed and cook until tender. They may be frozen and enjoyed during the cold winter months.

My Aunt Velma died the first day of January in 1926. My uncle kept the children at home until it was time to start his crop; then the youngest 4 children came to live with us. We now had 9 mouths to feed, so our garden really came in handy.

Before the potatoes were ready to harvest, we "grubbed" (to dig up by the roots) them with a table fork. We removed enough dirt to get the largest potatoes for eating. The smaller potatoes were left and covered back with dirt to grow larger. The spuds were stored under the house where it was cool. My mother would cook a gallon syrup bucket of potatoes every day.

Sometimes, we would make soup from our garden fresh vegetables, seasoned with butter and cream. Salt pork, if any left, was too old to use for seasoning.

With my uncle's help, his older children were able to make a home for all of their family by the time we moved to Oklahoma in 1928.

We kept sweet potatoes covered with sand in a box behind the cook stove so they wouldn't freeze.

When in season, this recipe was a quick easy dish that my mother fixed when we came in from the cotton patch. I can still smell the aroma of the cinnamon.

MY MOTHER'S FRIED SWEET POTATOES
circa 1920

Cut sweet potatoes lengthwise about 1/8 inch thick. Fry in butter for about 10 minutes with lid. Remove lid and sprinkle with sugar and cinnamon. The sugar will help brown them. Cook until tender.

SWEET POTATO PYE
circa 1908

2 cups boiled sweet potato
2 Tbsp. butter
2 Tbsp. lemon juice
1 cup sugar
grated rind of 1/2 lemon
1 Tbsp. ginger
1 Tbsp. cinnamon
pinch of salt
1/2 grated nutmeg
2 cups sugar
3 egg yolks
3 egg whites

Rub potatoes through a sieve, add butter, lemon juice, sugar in which has been mixed with grated lemon rind, ginger, cinnamon, salt and grated nutmeg. Stir well. Add milk and the beaten egg yolks. Egg whites beaten stiff are added last. Fit the paste to pan, dust with flour, fill and bake in unbaked crust. (There are no cooking directions when using a woodstove. You had to use your own judgement)

AUNT BURNICE'S CANDIED SWEET POTATOES

6 medium size sweet potatoes
1 cup corn syrup
1/2 cup sugar (brown sugar is good)
1/4 tsp. salt
4 Tbsp. butter

Put 6 med. size sweet potatoes in boiling water, cool and skin. Cut in halves, lengthwise unless too large, then slice in thirds. Put in casserole dish large enough to pack one layer.

Make a syrup from sugar and corn syrup. Add salt and butter, cook until fairly thick. Pour over potatoes and bake at 325° for 1 hour.

YAM MALLOW CRISP
in memory of Effie O. Talley

1 lb. can of yams with juice
1/8 cup orange juice
1/4 cup flour
1/4 cup sugar
1 tsp. cinnamon
a dash of salt
1/4 cup margarine
3/4 cup marshmallows

Place yams in baking dish, and pour orange juice over them. Combine flour, sugar, cinnamon and salt. Mix well. Cut in margarine until mixture resembles coarse crumbs. Sprinkle over yams. Bake at 350° for 30 minutes. Sprinkle with marshmallows and put under broiler to brown.

Lou Allen, my mother-in-law, was a good cook, homemaker and the mother of 7 children (6 boys, 1 girl in the middle). She was of the old school when it came to recipes; she had very few. Her apple dumplings was a favorite among her family.

LOU ALLEN'S BOILED APPLE DUMPLINGS
circa 1890

SYRUP:
1/2 cup lt. brown sugar (packed)
1/4 cup butter
1/4 tsp. salt

DUMPLINGS:
1 tsp. lemon juice
1 cup flour
2 tsp. baking powder
2 Tbsp. sugar
1/4 tsp. salt
1/3 cup milk + 1 Tbsp. milk
4 cups tart apples (finely diced)

For the syrup, measure the first 3 ingredients into a 3 quart saucepan. Boil for about 3 minutes. Mix flour, baking powder, salt, 2 Tbsp. sugar with enough milk to make a stiff batter. Add by tsp. to the boiling syrup. Add apples to the syrup. Add the dumplings last. Simmer slowly for about 20 minutes or less, until dumplings are done. Remove from heat and let stand for 10 minutes. Serve warm with whipped cream.

The old time cooks rarely used any thickening in fruit pies. They used baking powder in the pastry, which produced a thick, puffy and porous crust. The inside layer of crust soaked up much of the fruit juice. The juice that was left was clear and very tasty, more so than the ones made with thickened corn starch.

Thank God for Dirty Dishes

Thank God for dirty dishes,

They have a lot to tell

While other folks go hungry,

We are so very well.

With home and health

and happiness,

We shouldn't want to fuss

For by this stack of evidence,

God's very good to us.

DESSERTS

My mother never made angel cakes, and after reading these instructions you'll understand why.

HOW TO BAKE AN ANGEL CAKE IN A WOOD BURNING STOVE

Put dough in ungreased pan; you want the cake to stick firmly. Study your oven to see if bakes good and brown under bottom. If cake does not crust under bottom, it will fall out when inverted and shrink in the fall. Put cake in moderately hot oven, and here you must use judgement -- hot enough for biscuits, too hot for butter cake. Experience can only teach you on this point. If you see cake browning before it rises to the top of the pan, throw your oven door open and let cold air rush in and cool the oven instantly. Be not afraid, the cold air will not hurt the cake; 2 seconds will cool oven; watch cake closely, don't be afraid to open door every 3 or 4 minutes. This is the only way to properly bake the cake. When the cake has raised above the top of the pan, increase your heat and finish baking rapidly. It will bake in about 25 minutes and should not take longer. Baking too long dries out moisture and makes the cake tough and dry. Watch carefully at this stage and take out of oven the moment it shrinks back to level. Invert pan. Rest on center tube and let hang in pan until cool. Then cut cake around the sides and center tube. Then with knife handle, knock back the slide on pan and run knife under cake on both sides. Turn out. Sponge cake should be baked just like angel cake.

In earlier days, people called Angel Food Cake just Angel Cake.

MRS. MILLS' ANGEL CAKE

1 1/2 cups egg whites
1 1/2 tsp. cream of tartar
1 cup cake flour
1 1/2 cup sugar
1 tsp. vanilla
a dash of salt
1/4 tsp. almond extract

Beat egg whites with a flat wire wisk by hand. This puts more air into eggs than a rotary beater. When slightly beaten, add cream of tartar over eggs. Beat until stiff and will stand in peaks. Sift flour, sugar and salt together several times. Gently fold into egg whites a little at a time from sifter. Add flavoring last. Bake in angel cake pan at 350° for 1 hour. When done turn pan upside down and immediately to cool. A bottle works really well to stand the cake on.

Mrs. Mills, my sister's mother-in-law, cut this cake by pulling sewing thread held between her thumb and forefinger on both hands and drawn through the cake. No electric knives in those days.

KITCHEN KAPERS: When shelling nuts, pecans or Brazil nuts, place 1 cup of nuts in 1 cup of water in 1 quart casserole dish and cook for 4 to 5 minutes. The nuts will come out whole.

This cake was made for me as a Christmas gift for 30 years by a neighbor, Maude Rogers.

TEXAS PECAN CAKE
in memory of Maude Rogers

1 lb. butter
1 lb. brown sugar
1 lb. pecans
1/2 lb. candied pineapples
1/2 lb. candied cherries
4 cups flour
1 tsp. baking powder
1 1/2 tsp. lemon extract
6 eggs (separated)

Cream butter and sugar. Add eggs one at a time; beating after each addition. This is the only liquid. Beat well. Gradually add 2 cups flour with baking powder. Use other 2 cups flour to dredge fruits and nuts. Add fruits, nuts and extract. Fold in well beaten egg whites. Place in well greased stem cake pan in refrigerator overnight before cooking. Bake at 325° for nearly 3 hours or until done.

KITCHEN KAPERS: For baking in oven-proof glass, lower temperature 25° to keep from overheating.

This recipe was given to me by a lady in a nearby community, Martha, Oklahoma, when I was a bride. Soon after she moved away, and I never remembered her name. So I called the cake - "Martha Cake."

MARTHA CAKE
the Best ever

2 cups sugar
1 cup butter
2 cups flour
1 tsp. baking soda (added to flour)
2/3 cup milk
5 egg whites (beaten nearly stiff)
1/2 cup raisins
1/2 cup pecans (broken)

Cream butter and sugar until light and fluffy. Add flour with 1 tsp. baking soda, alternately with milk. Add rest of ingredients except eggs that you fold in last. Bake in 3 layers at 350° for 25 or 30 minutes or until done. Let cool and add filling.

FILLING

juice of 2 lemons
rind of 1 lemon
1/2 cup cream
1 cup coconut
2 egg yolks
4 Tbsp. flour
2 cups sugar

Mix in order given. Cook until thick. Can spread on top and between layers of spread between layers only and ice with 7 minute icing.

Minnie is 98 years old, and this recipe was used for her older sister's wedding cake. Minnie was our housekeeper for 15 years and a great cook.

MINNIE WHITE'S 1-2-3-4 POUND CAKE
circa 1895

1 cup butter
2 cups sugar
4 eggs (separated)
1/2 tsp. vanilla
1/2 tsp. almond extract
1 cup all purpose flour
2 tsp. baking powder

Have all ingredients at room temperature. Cream butter and sugar. Beat egg yolks and add to sugar mixture. Stir extracts into milk. Sift flour and baking powder twice and beat into sugar and butter mixture alternately with milk. Fold in stiffly beaten egg whites. Pour into well greased and floured 2 1/2 quart tube pan. Bake in preheated 350° oven for 50 minutes or until cake tests done.

AUNT BURNICE'S LAISY DAISY CAKE
circa 1940

2 eggs
1 cup sugar
1 cup flour
1/2 cup boiling milk
1 tsp. baking powder
1/4 tsp. salt
2 tsp. butter
1 tsp. vanilla

Beat eggs light with rotary beater, add sugar gradually and then stir in vanilla. Add flour, baking powder and salt, sifted together. Then add boiling milk, in which butter has melted, stirring all the time with a rotary egg beater. Pour in shallow greased pan, bake in a moderate oven about 375°.

ICING

Mix ingredients together:

9 tsp. brown sugar
5 tsp. melted butter
1/2 cup coconut

Spread over cake, which must be cooled in pan. Place under broiler and let stay until brown.

WESTERN CAKE
an old recipe found on a sugar box - a favorite with the men

1 box powdered sugar
3 sticks margarine
6 eggs
1 sugar box filled with sifted flour
1 tsp. lemon juice
1 tsp. vanilla

Cream butter, add sugar gradually. Beat until fluffy. Add eggs one at a time. Add flour gradually, then flavoring. Cook in greased stem pan at 325° for 1 1/2 hours. Invert to cool.

This recipe was given to me before World War II by a dear lady who lived to be 100 years old.

MRS. SKINNER'S OLD FASHIONED POUND CAKE

in memory of Ethel Skinner

1 cup butter (for best results, no
    substitute)
1 2/3 cups sugar
1 tsp. vanilla
1 tsp. lemon juice
grated rind of 1/2 lemon
2 cups flour
5 whole eggs

Cream butter until fluffy. Add sugar gradually and cream until fluffy like whipped cream. This is the foundation of your cake, so be sure it's done right. Add eggs one at a time, beating after each one until smooth. Sift flour with salt and divide into 4 portions, beating and folding until mixed. Do not stir. Do not overbeat. Stop when batter is smooth. Add flavoring. Place in oiled loaf pan, or tube pan is perfect. Bake at 350° for 50 minutes. Turn out on wire rack to cool. When cool, store in crock or stone jar.

KITCHEN KAPERS: When using bananas for cakes or bread, they should be fully ripe (real important). If there is even a hint of green at the tips, or if there are no brown flakes, it's better to make another kind of bread and wait for the bananas to ripen.

My sister-in-law, Zora Baker, made this cake everytime she visited us from California.

ZORA'S CARROT CAKE
in memory of Zora Baker

3 cups flour
2 cups sugar
2 tsp. baking powder
1 tsp. baking soda
2 tsp. cinnamon
1 1/2 cups pecans
1 cup Wesson Oil
2 cups carrots (grated)
1 can (no. 303) crushed pineapple with
     juice
2 tsp. vanilla
3 eggs

Sift and mix dry ingredients. Add liquids, then nuts. Add beaten eggs last. Bake in 3 - 9 inch cake pans well greased at 350° for 25 to 30 minutes until done.

FILLING

1 box powdered sugar
1 stick margarine (room temp.)
1 package (8 oz.) cream cheese
     (room temp.)
1 tsp. vanilla

Cream well and spread between layers, top and sides. Cover and refrigerate. You may add 1 cup coconuts and 1/2 cup nuts.

RED EARTH CAKE
in memory of Nell Tims

1/2 cup margarine
1 1/2 cup sugar
1 egg
4 Tbsp. cocoa
1 tsp. red food coloring
2 Tbsp. strong hot coffee
2 cups flour
1/4 tsp. salt
1 tsp. baking soda
1 cup fresh buttermilk
1 tsp. vanilla

Cream margarine and sugar until light and fluffy. Blend in egg which has been beaten until light and fluffy. Mix cocoa, coloring and hot coffee to smooth paste. Stir into creamed mixture. Sift flour and measure with salt and soda. Add alternately with buttermilk. Bake in 2 layers at 350° for 30 to 35 minutes. Ice with favorite icing.

CHESS CAKE

2 sticks margarine (soft)
2 cups sugar
6 eggs
2 cups flour
1/2 tsp. vanilla

Cream margarine and sugar. Add eggs one at a time, beating well. Add flour, a pinch of salt and vanilla. Beat well. Bake at 350° for 45 to 50 minutes. Keeps good in freezer.

I ate this cake for the first time in a restaurant in Washington, D.C., in the mid-50's. I've been looking for this recipe ever since and have just found it.

NEW YORK CREAM CHEESE POUND CAKE

Cream together:

3 sticks margarine
1 package (8 oz.) cream cheese

ADD:

3 cups sugar
a dash of salt
1 1/2 tsp. vanilla
6 large eggs (one at a time)
3 cups flour (sifted)

Bake in greased tube pan at 350° oven for 1 1/2 hours.

COATING RECIPE FOR CAKE PANS

This is a coating you'll be happy to have when the directions say "grease well and flour," and was used before we had commercial sprays to coat pans.

1 1/4 cup shortening
1/4 cup flour
1/4 cup salad oil

Mix until creamy. Do not heat or cook. Use a pastry brush or a piece of paper towel to coat cake pans before using. Fingers will work. Store mixture in airtight containers in refrigerator.

ITALIAN CREAM CAKE
one of my favorite cakes
in memory of Winfred Vernon

1 stick margarine
1/2 cup vegetable shortening
2 cups sugar
5 egg yolks
2 cups flour
1 tsp. baking soda
1 tsp. vanilla
1 cup buttermilk
1 small can coconut
1 cup chopped nuts

Cream fat and sugar, beat until light. Add egg yolks, one at a time. Sift dry ingredients. Add salt in milk. Stir in vanilla, nuts and coconut. Pour batter in 3 square greased and floured pans 9 x 9 inches. Bake at 350° for 25 minutes.

CREAM CHEESE FILLING

1 package (8oz.) cream cheese (room temp.)
1 stick margarine
1 box powdered sugar
a dash of salt
1 tsp. vanilla
1/2 cup chopped nuts

Mix well and beat good. Spread over cooled cake. Refrigerate.

KITCHEN KAPERS: Add cinnamon and nutmeg to custard and nutmeg to peach cobblers.

SAUERKRAUT CAKE

1/2 cup butter
1 1/2 cup sugar
3 eggs
1 tsp. vanilla
3 cups flour
1 tsp. baking powder
1 tsp. baking soda
1/4 tsp. salt
1/2 cup cocoa
1 cup water
1 cup sauerkraut (rinsed, drained and
     finely chopped)

Cream butter, add sugar, then eggs one at a time. Stir all dry ingredients together and add to the creamed mixture alternately with water. Stir in sauerkraut. Bake at 350° for 35 to 40 minutes in a sheet cake pan. Frost with sour cream frosting.

AUNT LELA'S DEVIL FOOD CAKE

Cream 1 cup shortening, 2 cups sugar and 3 eggs. Add alternately, 3 cups flour, 1 cup buttermilk and 2 tsp. vanilla. Add last, 1/2 cup cocoa, 1 rounded tsp. of baking soda and 1/2 cup boiling water. Bake at 350°. Makes 3 layers.

KITCHEN KAPERS: In making cakes where buttermilk or molasses are lacking, use a cup of applesauce with a tsp. of soda. Besides being a good substitute, the sauce makes a delicious spice cake without eggs.

BLIND DATE CAKE
in memory of Joyce Tipton

1 cup dates (cut fine)
1 1/4 cup boiling water
1 tsp. baking soda
1/2 cup shortening
1 cup sugar
2 eggs (beaten)
1 tsp. vanilla
1 1/4 cups flour
3 tsp. cocoa
1/2 tsp. salt

TOPPING

1/2 cup sugar
2/3 cup chocolate chips
1/2 cup chopped nuts

Pour water over dates. When cool, mash and add baking soda. Cream shortening, sugar, eggs and vanilla. Sift flour, cocoa and salt. Combine all the ingredients and pour in a greased flat pan. Sprinkle topping on batter and press down. Bake at 325° for 35 minutes.

KITCHEN KAPERS: When using lemons in a recipe that doesn't use the rind, pare off the yellow portion carefully, put through a meat chopper with the finest plate and spread out to dry. Then put in airtight container. This is really nice to have when no fresh lemon is available. Grate before you remove juice. It's easier that way. Drying is the secret.

JEWISH NEW YEAR HONEY CAKE

1/4 lb. butter
1 cup sugar (sifted)
3/4 cup honey
3 eggs
2 1/2 cups flour
2 tsp. baking powder
2 tsp. baking soda
1/2 tsp. salt
1 tsp. cinnamon
1/2 tsp. cloves
1/2 tsp. nutmeg
1/3 cup liquid coffee (cold)
1/3 cup blackberry wine
3/4 cup chopped walnuts

Preheat oven to 350°. Cream butter and sugar and blend well. Add honey and eggs one at a time, beating well after each addition. Sift flour and all ingredients together. Blend coffee and wine. Add flour mixture alternately with coffee and wine. When well blended fold in nuts. Pour batter into a well greased and lightly floured 9 to 10 inch tube pan or bundt pan. Bake at 350° for 45 minutes. Serves 15. The traditional greeting for the Jewish New Year is "Have a sweet year."

KITCHEN KAPERS: When greasing and flouring a pan for chocolate cake to keep from sticking, dust with cocoa instead of flour to prevent the white spots on bottom of cake.

JENNIE'S DEVILS FOOD CAKE
in memory of Jennie Thrash

1 3/4 cup sugar
1/2 cup Crisco
1/2 cup cocoa dissolved in enough
        water to make a cup
1/2 cup buttermilk
1 heaping tsp. baking soda
1 large egg or 2 small ones
1 tsp. vanilla
2 scant cups flour

ICING

2 cups sugar
2 Tbsp. cocoa
2 Tbsp. Karo syrup (white)
2 Tbsp. butter
1 tsp. vanilla
enough milk to mix good

Mix Crisco, sugar and egg. Beat until smooth. Add cocoa mixed in hot water, then add milk with soda dissolved in it. Add pinch of salt, vanilla and flour. Mix well. Pour into a loaf pan. Bake at 350° about 25 minutes or until done.

ICING

Mix sugar, cocoa and syrup with enough milk to mix good. Cook until it boils over skillet. Set in cold water, add butter and 1/2 tsp. vanilla. Let cool a while, beat until creamy and add to cake.

PRUNE CAKE
in memory of Gladys Brown

1 1/4 cup Wesson Oil
1 1/2 cup sugar
1 cup prunes (cooked and pitted)
1/4 cup prune juice
1 cup pecans (chopped)
1 cup buttermilk
1 tsp. baking soda
1 tsp. salt
1/2 tsp. cinnamon
1/2 tsp. allspice
1 tsp. vanilla
3 eggs
2 cups flour (sifted)
Mix all ingredients given in order by hand. Bake in 2 greased cake pans (9 inches) at 350° for 25 to 30 minutes. Cool before icing.

ICING

1 cup sugar
1 1/2 cup buttermilk
1/2 tsp. baking soda
2 Tbsp. butter

Mix all ingredients and boil to soft boil stage. Beat slightly. Spread on cake while icing is still warm.

KITCHEN KAPERS: To soften hard lumps of brown sugar, put into airtight containers with a slice of bread for a few days.

MINNIE WHITE'S BANANA NUT CAKE
my son's favorite

1 1/2 cups sugar
1/2 cup shortening
2 eggs
2 cups flour
2 tsp. baking soda
1 1/4 cups bananas
1/2 cup pecans (chopped)
1 tsp. vanilla
a dash of salt
6 Tbsp. buttermilk

Cream sugar and shortening. Add eggs one at a time and beat. Sift flour, baking soda and salt. Add dry ingredients alternating with milk and creamed mixture. Add mashed bananas, pecans and vanilla. Mix. Bake in 2 greased and floured 9 inch cake pans. Bake at 375° for 30 minutes and let cool.

FROSTING

1 box powdered sugar
1/4 lb. butter
1 ripe banana (mashed)
1 Tbsp. heavy cream
1 tsp. vanilla
1/2 cup pecans

Mix in order given and spread on cake. Refrigerate.

MARIE MILLS' CHOCOLATE CHERRY CAKE

1 pkg. Pillsbury Plus Devil's
    Food Cake Mix
3 eggs
21 oz. can prepared cherry pie filling
1 tsp. bitter almond extract

Preheat oven to 350°. Grease and flour 12 cup bundt, tube or 13 x 9 x 2 inch pan. In large bowl, blend first 4 ingredients until moistened. Beat 2 minutes at highest speed. Pour into prepared pan. Bake 40 to 50 minutes, until toothpick inserted in center comes out clean. Cool in pan 25 minutes and turn out on serving plate. Cool completely.

GLAZE

1/2 cup semi-sweet chocolate chips
1 Tbsp. butter or margarine
1 Tbsp. milk
1/2 cup powdered sugar

Blend first 3 ingredients over low heat, stirring constantly, until chocolate pieces melt. Remove from heat, stir in powdered sugar until smooth. Add additional milk, if necessary for glaze consistency. Spoon over cooled cake.

"Where there is no vision, the people perish; but he that keepeth the law, happy is he."
Proverbs 29:18

MARIE MILLS' BETTER THAN ANYTHING CAKE

1 box Duncan Hines Butter Cake Mix
1 (20 oz.) can pineapple (crushed)
1 cup sugar
1 pkg. instant vanilla pudding (3 oz.)
1 cup flake coconut
1 carton (8oz.) whipped topping
1 cup chopped nuts

Bake cake as directed in a 13 x 9 x 2 inch pan. Meanwhile, simmer pineapple and sugar. Remove cake from oven, punch holes in top and cover with pineapple. Mix instant pudding as directed on box, add coconut. Spread over pineapple. Cover with whipped topping and sprinkle with nuts.

RAW APPLE CAKE
in memory of Nova Crow

2 cups sugar
1/2 cup shortening
1 cup boiling water
2 eggs
3 cups flour
1 Tbsp. cocoa
1 tsp. cloves, allspice
1 1/2 tsp. baking soda
a dash of salt
1 1/2 cups raw apples (peeled & diced)
1 cup nuts
1 cup raisins

Pour boiling water over sugar and shortening, beating gradually. Sift dry ingredients (save 1/2 cup flour to dredge fruit and nuts). Add unbeaten eggs one at a time, then flour. Bake at 350° in 2 or 3 pans. Frost with favorite filling or can bake in a bundt pan and glaze with chocolate.

APPLE GOODIE

Ruth Russell
a 3rd generation recipe

3 cups of apples (sliced)
1 cup white sugar
1 Tbsp. flour
1/2 - 1 tsp. cinnamon

Mix ingredients and place in bottom of a buttered and floured baking pan. Top with the following:

3/4 cup oatmeal
3/4 cup flour
3/4 cup brown sugar
1/2 tsp. baking soda
1/2 tsp. baking powder
1/4 tsp. salt
1 cup butter or margarine

Mix together and spread over apples. It will be crumbly. Bake at 350° for 45 minutes, or until apples are done.

The above recipe by Ruth Russell (grandmother) was furnished by Virgie Hern (mother) and Debbie Mills (granddaughter).

Our colonial predecessors, armed only with a heavy iron pot, an open fireplace and the bounty brought in from the field and forest, turned their meals into feasts that are chronicled in today's history. Such is the case with old recipes done up with a new flavor, like the old time Burnt Sugar Cake. I can recall one of my mother's cousins, Ethel Trevathan, cooking breakfast on a wood stove, while her husband, Joyce, cooked burnt sugar syrup on the fireplace. The syrup was really good with real butter and hot biscuits.

BURNT SUGAR CAKE

2 cups cake flour (sifted)
1 1/2 cups sugar
1 Tbsp. baking powder
1 tsp. salt
1/2 cup oil (butter flavor)
6 eggs (separated)
1/3 cup burnt sugar syrup (recipe
        below)
1/4 cup water (cold)
1 1/2 tsp. vanilla
1/2 tsp. cream of tartar

Sift flour, sugar, baking powder and salt into mixing bowl. Make a "well" and add oil, egg yolks, burnt sugar syrup, cold water and vanilla. Beat until smooth. Beat egg whites and cream of tartar until very stiff peak form. Pour batter over beaten egg whites and gently fold together until just blended. Pour into ungreased tube pan. Bake at 350° for 1 hour, or until top springs back when lightly touched. Invert on funnel or neck of tall bottle. Let hang until cold. Remove from pan. Frost top with burnt sugar icing, allowing icing to dribble down sides; decorate with walnut or pecan halves.

BURNT SUGAR SYRUP

In heavy skillet over low heat. Melt 1 cup sugar until clear and amber color. Remove from heat; slowly stir in 1/2 cup of boiling water. Return to heat and cook, stirring occasionally until lumps melt and syrup is smooth. Cool thoroughly before using. Use 1/3 cup syrup for cake and reserve remaining syrup for icing.

BURNT SUGAR ICING

Beat 2 cups powdered sugar (sifted), reserved burnt sugar syrup, 2 Tbsp. of cream and 1 tsp. vanilla together until smooth. Add more cream if icing is too thick to spread smoothly.

This cake was made by Debbie Mills' great grandmother, Eva Davis, for Debbie's great aunt's wedding. This recipe is at least 100 years old. Debbie is Marie Mills' daughter-in-law.

LADY DAVIS CAKE
in memory of Eva Sarah Lyons Davis
100 year old recipe

1 cup butter
2 cups sugar
1 cup milk
3 1/2 cups flour
2 tsp. baking powder
vanilla or lemon flavoring
6-8 egg whites (add later)

Mix ingredients together and then fold in 6 to 8 egg whites which have been beaten until stiff. Bake at 350°.

SAUCES FOR CAKES AND PUDDINGS
from an old 1910 cookbook

LEMON SAUCE
circa 1910

1 cupful sugar
1/2 cupful water
yolks of 3 eggs
rind and juice of 2 lemons

Boil the water, sugar, juice and rind of lemons all together for 10 minutes. Beat the egg yolks. Strain the syrup and stir the eggs into it. Set the saucepan in boiling water and beat rapidly until thick and smooth. Remove from the water and beat 5 minutes.

ORANGE SAUCE
circa 1910

1 cupful sugar
1 cupful water
1/2 tsp. cornstarch
3/4 cupful orange juice
juice of 1 lemon
1 cupful orange pulp

Make a syrup of sugar and water and thicken with cornstarch. Take from fire, cool and add orange juice, juice of lemon and orange pulp. Serve ice cold.

MAPLE SAUCE
circa 1910

1/4 lb. maple sugar
1/2 cupful water
whites of 2 eggs
1 cupful thick cream
1 tsp. vanilla

Boil water and sugar 'til it will spin. Whisk boiling hot into the beaten egg whites. Add cream and vanilla.

CHOCOLATE SAUCE
circa 1910

1 cupful water
1 cupful sugar
1 stick cinnamon
1 square Runkel's chocolate
1/2 cupful milk
1 1/2 Tbsp. cornstarch
pinch of salt
1 tsp. McIlhenny's Mexican Vanilla

Cook together the water, sugar and cinnamon. Strain. Add the chocolate which has been dissolved in hot milk, thickened with cornstarch and a little water. Add the salt and beat until creamy. After taking off the fire, add the vanilla and serve hot. This is a very nice sauce with a hot plain pudding of any kind or with vanilla ice cream frozen hard.

MRS. MILLS' FAVORITE SAUCE

Cream 1/3 cup powdered sugar with 2 Tbsp. butter at room temperature. Beat the yolks until lemon color and then beat into sugar mixture. Beat the egg whites until stiff. Fold in mixture and cook over real low heat until thickens. It will be foamy (never boil). Stir constantly. When cool, add your favorite flavoring, lemon, orange, rum, etc. It's very good to "dress up" leftover cake, bread pudding, or just about anything you can dream up.

106

LEMON BUTTER SAUCE

1 large egg
1 lemon (juice and grated rind)
1 cup sugar
2 Tbsp. butter

Mix all ingredients in top of double boiler. Cook over low heat, stirring occasionally with balloon whisk until it thickens and clarifies. Good with waffles, pancakes or toast. In the earlier days it was "pass the biscuits, please."

We were in trouble when there was a pie supper at the schoolhouse to raise money for a family that lost everything by fire. We had no eggs to make pies, since the hens were not laying because of moulting (losing their feathers). We always had guineas; they were from a wild specie of fowl. They would hide their nests is odd places. They made good watch dogs at night. If a strange dog, or even a wolf or skunk got too close to the barn or hen house, they would make a "nervous cackle." My father searched high and low looking for their nests and came back to the house with his hat full of guinea eggs. He surprised us with the eggs and saved the day. I remember how happy he was that we could go the pie supper.

The guinea egg whites wouldn't beat into meringue, so my mother came up with this buttermilk pie made from real butter, fresh buttermilk and lemon extract.

MY MOTHER'S BUTTERMILK PIE
a custard pie with a delicate sweet
tartness of a good cheesecake

1 cup sugar
3 Tbsp. flour
1/4 tsp. salt
3 egg yolks (slightly beaten)
3 egg whites
2 cups buttermilk (freshly churned)
1 tsp. lemon extract

Combine the sugar, flour, salt and blend thoroughly. Beat egg yolks slightly and add buttermilk, lemon extract and butter that has been melted and cooled. Add gradually to dry ingredients and blend thoroughly. Fold in stiffly-beaten egg whites, gently but thoroughly. Pour into unbaked pie shell. Bake at 450° for 10 minutes and reduce to 300°. Bake until knife inserted in center comes out clean. Cool on wire cake rack. (I have added instructions for today's oven, but in a woodstove you would need a moderately slow oven.)

EGG CUSTARD PIE
recipe has been in my family for 60 years

5 eggs
1 quart milk
1 tsp. nutmeg
2 pie shells (unbaked)
1 1/2 cups sugar
1 tsp. vanilla
1 Tbsp. flour

Beat eggs, add sugar and mix thoroughly. Add milk, vanilla, nutmeg, flour, and blend well. Pour into 2 unbaked pie shells. Bake at 325° for 30 to 40 minutes or until custard has set. Serves 12.

KITCHEN KAPERS: After an apple pie is baked (while still hot), slice back the top crust and add a thin slice of cheese. Mrs. Mills said, "Apple pie without cheese is like a hug without a squeeze."

I feel sorry for people who have never eaten this pie. I've made this pie for fifty years.

PEACH CUSTARD PIE
in memory of Thel Woods

3 eggs beaten well, gradually beat in sugar. Add pinch of salt (the amount you can hold between finger and thumb). Add 2 Tbsp. of melted butter before putting custard in pie shell. Peel enough free stone peaches in halves to fill the bottom of unbaked pie shell. Place seed side up. Use ripe peaches or canned halves can be substituted. Pour egg mixture over peaches in pie shell. Start at 400° for 10 minutes, and reduce to 325° for 30 minutes or until custard is set.

MYSTIC PIE

20 Ritz crackers
1 cup sugar
1/2 tsp. baking powder
3 egg whites
1 cup pecans (chopped)
1 tsp. vanilla
1 cup heavy cream

Crunch crackers fine. Add 1/2 cup sugar. Beat egg whites until stiff. Slowly beat in 1/2 cup sugar. Combine crumbs and egg whites. Add nuts and vanilla, blend well. Pour into a well greased pie pan. Bake at 350° for 30 minutes. Top with whipped cream when ready to serve. Chill.

Just 4 ingredients - the easiest pie you'll ever make.

APRICOT PIE

Stir 1/2 cup sour cream in 1 can (16oz.) of apricot pie filling until almost blended. Turn in a 9 inch graham cracker crust. Sprinkle 1 cup flaked coconut, toasted over filling. Chill thoroughly for at least 4 hours.

SOUR CREAM APPLE CAKE

Combine 1/2 cup granulated sugar, 1 Tbsp. flour, 1/2 tsp. salt, 1/4 tsp. cinnamon, and 1/4 tsp. nutmeg. Toss with 6 cups pared, cored, sliced tart apples. Arrange in unbaked 9 inch pastry shell. Cover loosely with foil. Bake in hot oven at 400° for 50 to 55 minutes or until apples are tender. Remove foil. Combine 1 cup dairy sour cream and 1/4 cup brown sugar. Pour evenly over apples. Sprinkle with nutmeg. Bake for 2 to 3 minutes longer.

CHESS PIE
Mrs. J. A. Southall
100+ years old recipe

4 egg yolks
3/4 cup sugar
6 Tbsp. butter
1/2 tsp. lemon extract
1/2 tsp. vanilla extract

Beat the egg yolks well. Cream sugar and butter together. Then add to this the yolks and the flavorings and beat well. Bake slowly in uncooked pie shell. It takes about 1 hour in a slow oven (200° to 250°). For one 8 inch pie.

PEANUT BUTTER PIE

2/3 cups sugar
2 1/2 Tbsp. cornstarch
1 Tbsp. flour
1/2 tsp. salt
3 cups milk
1 Tbsp. butter
3 slightly beaten egg yolks
1/4 cup peanut butter (crunchy)
3 egg whites (meringue)

Combine sugar, cornstarch, flour and salt in saucepan. Add milk and cook over low heat, stirring constantly until mixture thickens and boils. Cook 2 more minutes. Remove from heat and stir a small amount of hot mixture into beaten egg yolks. Return to hot mixture. Cook 1 more minute, stirring constantly. Add peanut butter. Stir until blended. Pour into 9 inch pie crust (baked). Top with meringue.

MRS. MILLS' FRENCH APPLE PIE
the Best apple pie ever

Peel and slice enough tart apples to fill and unbaked pie shell. Sprinkle 1/2 sugar over apples. Sprinkle cinnamon over apples if desired. For top crust, whip 1/2 cup brown sugar, 1/2 cup butter and 1/2 cup flour until of whipped cream consistency. Spread on top of apples. Start baking at 450° for 10 minutes and reduce to 350° until apples are done.

This recipe is over 100 years old and originated in the Minor family with Mrs. Southall's father Hugh Minor, Sr. He would first make a white cake using egg whites and then make the chess pie from the yolks. Mr. Minor's white cake is next.

WHITE CAKE

Mrs. J. A. Southall
100+ years old recipe

8 egg whites
1 cup butter
2 cups sugar
1 tsp. vanilla
1 cup milk
3 tsp. (level) baking powder
a dash of salt
3 cups flour

Cream butter and sugar. Add vanilla. Sift flour, salt and baking powder 2 times. Beginning and ending with flour, alternate with milk 3 or 4 times into creamed sugar and butter. Beat and mix well. Beat whites until stiff. Fold whites into other mixture carefully. Pour into 9 x 13 inch oblong pan or a tube pan or 3 round pans, greased and floured. Bake at 350°.

SOUTHERN STYLE RAISIN PIE

in memory of Mrs. Green Cotney
pre-Civil War recipe

Gradually add 1 cup sugar to two beaten eggs. Add 6 Tbsp. melted butter and 1/4 cup milk. Stir in 1 cup raisins and 1/2 cup broken pecans. Pour in unbaked pie shell. Bake at 350° for 40 to 45 minutes. Serve with whipped cream.

112

OMA'S PECAN PIE
Oma Voorhies

2 1/2 cups maple syrup
1/2 scant cup sugar
4 Tbsp. butter
4 eggs (beaten)
dash of salt
1 tsp. vanilla
1 1/2 cup nuts

Add butter, maple syrup, sugar and boil gently for 3 to 5 minutes. Cool slightly and pour in 4 beaten eggs. Add dash of salt and vanilla to mixture. Put in 1 1/2 cup of nuts in bottom of the raw crust. Pour the mixture over nuts. Bake 10 minutes at 450°, then 30 minutes at 350°. Makes 2 pies.

MARIE MILLS' BUTTERSCOTCH PIE

2 cups granulated sugar
1/4 lb. butter
1 quart sweet milk (heated)
3 egg yolks
2 Tbsp. cornstarch
1/2 cup water
1 tsp. vanilla (real vanilla is best)

Brown the sugar in melted butter, stirring constantly and gradually add the hot milk. When it begins to thicken, slowly add the slightly beaten egg yolks and the cornstarch (dissolved in small amt. water). Stir until thick. Pour into bake shell. Cover with meringue. Makes 2 pies.

These pies have gone to school in many lunch boxes.

SOUTHERN FRIED PIES

2 cups flour
2 tsp. baking powder
1/2 tsp. salt
3 Tbsp. lard
3/4 cup milk
cooked fruit of any kind (I prefer dried apricots)
fat for frying

Mix dry ingredients and cut in lard, gradually add milk, making a dry dough. Toss on a floured dough board and knead lightly. Roll about 1/4 inch thick and cut into circles, using a saucer for a pattern. Place less than 2 Tbsp. of fruit, well drained, on half of the circle. Moisten the edges with cold water and press together with the tines of a fork. Fry pies in shallow hot fat until brown, turning them several times. Remove from fat and drain of soft paper. You may have to add a little more fat between frying.

MRS. MILLS' LEMON PYE
circa 1910

Mix 1 heaped Tbsp. of flour or slightly less of cornstarch with 3/4 cup sugar and scant 1/4 tsp. salt. Add the well beaten egg yolks of 3 eggs and white of one, the grated rind of half and juice of 1 large lemon and 1 1/2 cup of water. Bake it in plate lined with rich crust in a moderate oven. Beat whites of 2 eggs with 1/2 cup of powdered sugar until very stiff. Pile it roughly on pie and color it slightly in a moderate oven.

MERINGUE FOR CREAM PIES

3 egg whites (room temp.)
1/4 tsp. cream of tartar
1/3 cup + 2 tsp. sugar

For best results, beat with a whisk. Beat egg whites until frothy. Then add cream of tartar and beat until almost stiff. Add 1 Tbsp. of sugar at a time, beating well after each addition. Meringue should be stiff, glossy and stand in peaks that curve over slightly. Quickly pile it lightly onto the filling that has had time to cool in shell. Then quickly swirl the meringue all over the top, touching the pastry all around. This will keep the meringue from shrinking away from pastry while baking.

GRACE ALLEN'S OSGOOD PYE
my sister-in-law
a 80 year old recipe

3/4 cup seedless raisins
1 1/2 cup sugar
1 cup chopped nuts
2 eggs (separated)
3/4 cup butter
1 tsp. cinnamon
1/2 tsp. nutmeg
2 tsp. vinegar

Rinse, drain raisins and chop fine. Mix and cream butter with sugar and spices, thoroughly. Blend in lightly beaten egg yolks and vinegar. Stir in raisins and nuts. Fold in beaten egg whites. Turn into unbaked pie shell (9 inches). Bake in hot oven at 450° for 10 minutes. Reduce heat to 350° and bake for 30 to 35 minutes longer.

GORGEOUS PUMPKIN PIE
in memory of Hazel Vite

1 pastry shell (9", unbaked)
1 3/4 cup canned pumpkin
1 Tbsp. butter
3/4 cup light brown sugar
1 Tbsp. flour
2 eggs
1 tall can (1 2/3 cups) evaporated milk
1 tsp. cinnamon
1/2 tsp. ginger
1/8 tsp. nutmeg
1/2 tsp. salt
whipped cream
cheddar cheese

Heat pumpkin in saucepan for 10 minutes, stirring frequently, until pumpkin is somewhat dry. Remove from heat. Stir in butter. Combine brown sugar and flour, add to pumpkin. Blend spices, salt, water, add to pumpkin. Stir until well mixed. Pour into pastry lined pie pan. Bake in hot oven at 450° for 15 minutes. Reduce heat to 300° and bake for about 45 minutes longer. Cool. Garnish with whipped cream and pumpkins cut from cheddar cheese.

"The heart of the prudent getteth knowledge; and the ear of the wise seeketh knowledge."
Proverbs 18:15

HOMEMADE ICE CREAM

I've read ice cream was a treat reserved only for kings and queens. History tells us over 2000 years ago, runners brought snow from the top of the Italian Alps, and Caesar's cooks saturated this snow with wine, giving them a delicious dessert, only available to royalty. Aren't we glad we didn't live then?

Ice Cream was not invented by the Americans, and it's origin is unknown. Nancy Johnson, a New Jersey hostess, gets credit for making the first homemade ice cream by churning a custard mixture in a hand cranked freezer with ice and salt. She wasn't a bit more inventive than my mother was in 1926.

MY MOTHER'S ICE CREAM

Beat 2 eggs (separated, then together). Beat 1 cup sugar into the eggs gradually and add a pinch of salt and a little vanilla. Add 1 cup of cream to this mixture and finish filling a 1/2 gallon syrup bucket with milk, leaving 1/2 inch at the top. Then the syrup bucket was put in a larger bucket surrounded by ice and salt. We took the small bucket and turned it back and forth with our hands planted firmly on the bucket lid. We had to open the bucket several times and stir the frozen mixture from the sides, until it was ready to eat.

Ice cream was made on the front porch only on Saturday nights in the summertime; the only time we had ice. There was always a bed on the porch in the summer; when we got cold from eating ice cream, we jumped in bed and covered up. When we got warm, we got up and ate some more.

Somehow, I have to feel sorry for the kids who haven't had that kind of ice cream or the experience of making it. Most ice cream freezers now are electric. I still have a gallon and a half hand cranked freezer, and my grandson prefers it. We make it in the kitchen sink, but I think it would be more fun to make it on the back porch or under a shade tree. There was, however, no dasher to lick in my mother's syrup bucket method.

The method of making ice cream has never been changed. It no doubt, had to be the favorite American dessert -- maybe the whole world. Let's not neglect this tradition. It's so delightful and something grandmas can do with their grandchildren. They won't forget the pleasure of licking the dasher and the goodness of the first dish.

SNOW ICE CREAM

1 can milk (Eagle brand)
chocolate syrup

Add these ingredients to enough snow to make ice cream the desired consistency.

THELMA AND MARIE'S SNOW ICE CREAM

Add sugar, milk, a pinch of salt, vanilla, beaten egg and cream. Mix these ingredients together and stir in the snow. If we wanted more, we would mix more ingredients and run out and get more snow. It was good, goood, goooood!

BASIC ICE CREAM
(1 gallon)

4 eggs (separated)
1 large can Milnot
1 package instant Jell-o vanilla pudding
2 cups sugar
1/2 tsp. vanilla
a dash of salt

Beat egg yolks with electric mixer. Wash blades and then beat whites until stiff. Then mix eggs well. Add sugar and pudding to egg mixture, gradually. Then add Milnot. Put mixture in the refrigerator ahead of time to chill. Take out and finish filling freezer with milk, just to the rim. It's now ready to freeze.

If you object to the raw eggs, use the pudding you cook. Add 2 beaten eggs with 2 cups sugar and the evaporated milk to the pudding mix and cook according to directions on the pudding mix. Add about 2 cups milk and let cool. When ready to freeze, finish filling the freezer can to the rim. Stir well. Hand freeze.

You can use any desired flavor or pudding. Then add desired fresh fruit, such as peaches, strawberries, bananas, or pineapple. You may want to add more sugar, determined by the tartness of fruit.

PLAIN ICE CREAM WITH COFFEE FLAVOR
circa 1910

Add 1 quart of rich milk with 1 cup of strong clear coffee and put on to boil. Moisten 1/2 cup of sugar and 1 saltspoon of salt (the saltspoon is the one placed by the individual salt seller that is placed by each serving plate on the dining table) and 3 Tbsp. level measure of flour, with 1/4 cup of cold milk and stir into the boiling milk. Cook over boiling water for 20 minutes, stirring until thickened and smooth. Add 2 eggs beaten with another 1/2 cup sugar. Stir until egg is set. Strain and when cold, freeze. Use 3 parts of fine ice and 1 part of rock salt. 1/2 cup of cream or more will improve it, but it is good without, and will not taste of flour if well cooked. More eggs may be used, if liked richer.

ICE CREAM MADE IN REFRIGERATOR ICE TRAYS
early '30's

Ice cream make in the mechanical refrigerator is unheard of now with the mega-supermarkets just around the corner with reasonable prices, and every flavor you can imagine. When made in ice trays, we used evaporated milk or whipping cream and took it out of the trays when partially frozen and stirred. Then the mixture was put back in the tray to finish freezing. The fat globules in evaporated milk was smaller because of homogenization. When I first had a refrigerator we used top milk. When we drank milk (wasn't homogenized then) we shook the glass milk bottle to mix the cream. When buying milk at the store, we returned the washed empty milk bottles for a deposit.

Evaporated milk to whip in the old days was brought to boiling point either in the can or a double boiler, then chilled and whipped. Beat with a rotary beater, surrounded by ice. Heating evaporated some of the water and thickened the milk. These frozen desserts were used a lot during World War II. Fruit, either fresh or canned, was usually available. You could substitute syrup for sugar. I still make ice cream in the refrigerator, occasionally, and it is still just as good. Now, we only chill the milk to whip.

During World War II when sugar was rationed, we substituted syrup in sauces, fruit pies, and many other ways.

VELVET SHERBET
Mary Loucyle Self

1 quart milk
1 package small Jell-o (any flavor. I like orange)
1 cup boiling water
1 cup white Karo syrup
juice of 2 lemons
grated rind from 1 lemon

Mix and add milk last. It will look like buttermilk. When partially frozen in ice tray, remove and stir. Then refreeze and serve when frozen.

PINEAPPLE SHERBET

1 1/2 cups evaporated milk
1 cup sugar
a pinch of salt
1 cup water
2 Tbsp. lemon juice
2 1/2 cups pineapple (crushed)

Chill milk. Add sugar, salt, lemon juice to pineapple and water. Stir thoroughly and chill. Then add pineapple mixture to chilled milk. Freeze in a tray like any ice cream.

121

BANANA NUT ICE CREAM

7 eggs
1/4 tsp. salt
1 1/2 cups sugar
1 Tbsp. vanilla
1 cup white Karo syrup
1 cup pecans
1 pint whipping cream
2 ripe bananas (mashed fine)

Beat yolks and whites separately. Beat yolks until light in color. Beat whites until they stand in peaks. Add half of sugar and beat. Add rest of sugar to whites and beat, then add both egg mixtures together. Add Karo, cream, salt and vanilla. Pour into freezer, add bananas and nuts. Add enough milk to fill freezer. Freeze and let set 1 hour. Makes 1 gallon.

FRESH PEACH ICE CREAM

2 cups powdered milk
2 1/4 cups water
1 large can milk
3 Tbsp. Karo syrup
1 3/4 cups sugar or less
1 Tbsp. vanilla
2 lbs. fresh peaches (sweetened)
2 pints coffee cream

Mix above ingredients in freezer can and finish filling can with milk. Makes 1 gallon. This recipe can be used for other flavors.

PINEAPPLE ICE CREAM

8 eggs (beaten)
2 cups sugar
1/4 cup flour
1 tall can milk
1 can (no. 2) pineapples (crushed)
1 cup heavy cream
2 Tbsp. vanilla
a dash of salt

Mix flour and sugar; add to eggs. Add remaining ingredients in order. Finish filling freezer can with milk. Freeze.

PEPPERMINT ICE CREAM

1 package vanilla ice cream powder
1 tall can evaporated milk
1 can Eagle Brand milk
8 eggs
1 Tbsp. vanilla
4 cups crushed peppermint candy

Beat eggs. Add ice cream powder, Eagle Brand milk and vanilla, mixing thoroughly. Add candy and evaporated milk. Add enough whole milk to fill 1 1/2 gallon freezer. Freeze.

This is a really good dessert that Marie has used for 25 years.

MARIE MILLS' APPLE PUDDING

Cream these ingredients:

1 cup sugar
1/4 cup shortening
1 egg

Add:

1 cup flour
1 tsp. baking soda
2 cups raw apples (chopped small)
1 cup coconut
1/2 cup pecans
a pinch of salt
1 Tbsp. vanilla

Mix in order given. Bake in flat shallow pan at 350° until done. Cut in squares and serve with whipped cream. (before the days of Cool Whip)

BOILED CUSTARD
in memory of R. B. Perkins

3 eggs
1/2 cup sugar
a pinch of salt
1 quart milk
1 tsp. vanilla

Beat the eggs, add sugar and salt. Scald 1 quart milk. When hot, add eggs and sugar. Cook in double boiler until coats a spoon. When slightly cool, add vanilla. Serve cold in a cup with plain cake or sip without cake. This was a tradition at Christmas.

CHOCOLATE MOUSSE
a favorite recipe

1st LAYER:

1 cup flour
1 stick oleo
1 cup nut meats

Mix and put into a 9 x 13 inch pan.
Bake at 350° until brown.

2nd LAYER:

1 1/2 cups Cool Whip
1 cup powdered sugar
cream cheese (8 oz.) at room temp.

Mix with mixer and spread over cool
crust.

3rd LAYER:

1 large package instant vanilla pudding
1 large package instant chocolate
pudding
3 cups milk

Beat thoroughly.   Spread over 2nd
layer.   Top with remaining Cool Whip.
Refrigerate before serving.

BREAD PUDDING

2 cups milk
2 eggs
1 cup biscuit chunks
1/2 cup sugar (more if desired)
1/4 tsp. salt
2 lumps of butter
1/4 tsp. vanilla

Add sugar to milk and bring to scalding point. Remove from heat; add biscuit chunks, salt, vanilla, melted butter and beaten eggs. Put in greased baking dish. Bake at 325° for 30 to 40 minutes, or until inserted knife comes out clean.

For variety, my mother added about 2 tablespoons of cocoa to the sugar. Sometimes, she used about 3/4 cup of brown sugar melted into butter.

My mother made rice pudding using this recipe; she never used pineapple, but I do.

MAY ROGERS' RICE PUDDING

4 cups milk
2 Tbsp. butter
a pinch of salt
4 eggs (beaten)
1 tsp. vanilla
1 cup sugar
1 1/2 cups rice (cooked)
3/4 cup pineapple (drained and crushed) or
3/4 cup raisins

Scald milk and the rest of the ingredients. You can use pineapple juice to finish milk. Add beaten eggs last. Bake at 300° or until set. Never allow to boil.

This recipe was given to me at least 40 years ago by Mrs. Grover Herndon. She's been gone for 20 years. I'm sure this recipe is over 60 years old.

If you'll notice there are no marshmallows melted on top in this old recipe. In the first place they just added to the cost of the dish, and we lived 18 miles from the store.

SWEET POTATO PUDDING
Mrs. Grover Herndon

1/2 cups raisins (optional)
4 cups grated raw sweet potatoes (packed well)
1 1/2 cups sugar
1 cup milk
1 tsp. <u>each</u> of cinnamon, nutmeg and allspice
1/2 tsp. salt
2 eggs (beaten)
2 rounded Tbsp. butter (melted)

Mix in order given. Place in greased pan. Cook slowly for 1 1/2 hours or until set.

MARIE MILLS' LEMON JELL-O
light and fluffy - especially good for summer

1 small package lemon Jell-o
1 1/4 cup water (boiling)
3/4 cup sugar
juice of 2 lemons

Mix the above ingredients and set aside to partially chill. Fold 1 cup chilled Pet Milk (whipped) into the above mixture. Add lemon juice last and grated rind, if desired. Use large Pyrex pan lined with Graham cracker crumbs. Also put crumbs on top. Refrigerate several hours before serving. Good! Good! Good!

HOT CARAMEL DUMPLINGS

2 Tbsp. butter
1 1/2 cups brown sugar
1 1/2 cups boiling water
1/8 tsp. salt

Place all ingredients in saucepan. Boil gently while preparing dumpling dough.

DUMPLINGS:

1 1/4 cups flour
1/8 tsp. salt
1/3 cup sugar
1/2 tsp. vanilla
1 1/2 tsp. baking powder
2 tsp. butter
1/2 cup milk

Sift flour, sugar, salt and baking powder; cut in butter. Add milk, vanilla and mix thoroughly. Drop by large spoonfuls into sauce. Cover pan. Boil slowly for 20 minutes. Don't remove lid. Serve in bowl with a generous dab of ice cream on top.

KITCHEN KAPERS: Mrs. Mills' Hand Lotion (makes 1/2 pint). 2/3 cups bay rum or rose water and 1/3 cup glycerin. Mix good. For chapped hands. This lotion will make your hands so soft.

APPLE DUMPLING ROLLS
Debbie Mills

PIE CRUST

2 cups flour
1/2 cup Crisco
1/4 tsp. salt
water

Cut Crisco into flour. Add water until you have a pliable dough. Roll out on floured surface. Butter pie crust.

NOW ADD sliced apples mixed with cinnamon and sugar. Spread over pie dough and roll up. Slice and put in 9 x 13 inch pan.

SAUCE

2 cups water
1 1/2 cups sugar
1/2 stick oleo
1/2 tsp. cinnamon

Cook over stove until boils. Pour over apples for glaze.

Bake at 350° for 1 hour.

COOKIES

AND

CANDIES

My first transportation to school was horseback, riding outside the saddle behind my brother with my arms locked around his waist. With no covered Tupperware, wax paper and Ziploc bags to use, my mother packed our dinner as best she could in tin buckets (1/2 gallon syrup buckets) that were hung from the saddle horn. Dinner was packed from the breakfast table: sausage or ham between a biscuit and a hard cooked egg with the shell (it packed better that way). For fun we could have a contest to see who could peel the egg first after being cracked on our foreheads. It was lots of fun and didn't cost a thing. In season we had baked sweet potatoes, and there was always a fried pie. If we ran out if mincemeat or fruit for the fried pies, there was always cinnamon and sugar dotted with butter. The pie crust was made from biscuit dough that was mixed for breakfast. Sometimes we would have biscuits soaked with butter and syrup. These biscuits were really nice, because we didn't have sticky fingers, and we had no napkins. The salt for the hard cooked eggs was wrapped in a folded square from a newspaper.

We probably would have had milk to drink, but we had no way to carry it. At school we had cool water from a well. Everyone drank from the same tin cup, but my mother furnished us with a folded cup that we kept in our desk.

When there were 3 of us going to school, my father furnished us with horse and buggy. I remember crossing a creek about halfway home that was out of its banks. The water had receded some, but the horse had a hard time getting up the steep bank. My brother had my sister and me sit on our feet and hold our books on out laps, so they wouldn't get wet. We were so frightened and we cried. It must have been hard on our 15 year old brother. He was so good and kind to us and really tried to take care of us.

We usually didn't have snacks except for the tea cakes that we could smell before we got into the house from school. My mother kept them in a square tin box that soda crackers came in. I'm sure she doubled the recipe.

OLD TIMEY TEA CAKES
80 year old recipe

3 large eggs
2 cups flour
3 1/2 handfuls of sugar
1 tsp. baking powder
1 tsp. baking soda
a pinch of salt
1 tsp. of vanilla
scant 1/2 cup pure lard
scant 1/2 cup bacon drippings

Sift flour in a big bowl. Make a well in center of flour. Put all ingredients in the well. Make a stiff dough and cut out with a snuff glass. The thicker the dough, the softer the cookie. To make a crisp cookie, roll thin.

Mixing for biscuits, pie crust or just about anything that used flour and shortening was done with fingertips, and of course, the sweets, like cakes, were not.

Thelma and Marie

Pounds and pounds of these oatmeal cookies were shipped to our service men overseas in World War II. Sometimes, it took that package from home 6 weeks to 2 months to arrive on the front, and the cookies kept good and arrived in good shape. There were always enough cookies to divide with everyone.

MARIE MILLS' OATMEAL COOKIES

Mix in order given:

2 cups granulated sugar
1 box brown sugar
1 lb. margarine
4 eggs (beaten)
1 small box (25 cents) oatmeal (quick-cooking)
3 cups + scant 1/3 cup flour with salt
1 1/2 Tbsp. salt
1 1/2 Tbsp. baking soda

Add salt and baking soda to the flour. Add last 1 small box of quick-cooking oats and 1 large package of chocolate chips. This recipe makes a lot. You can freeze in rolls, slice and cook when needed. Bake at 350° for 10-12 minutes.

BUTTERSCOTCH PECAN COOKIES
a crispy cookie

1 stick oleo margarine
1 1/2 cups brown sugar (packed)
1 tsp. vanilla
1 cup flour
1 egg
1 cup pecans

Cream butter, sugar and add vanilla. Add egg and blend well. Add flour and nuts, mix until all flour is moistened. Drop by a teaspoon onto a baking sheet. Bake at 350° for about 12 minutes until done. If needed to moisten flour, add a little milk.

SAND TARTS
Fern Tims

1 stick oleo margarine
6 Tbsp. powdered sugar
2 cups flour (sifted)
a dash of salt
1 tsp. vanilla
1/2 tsp. almond
1 cup broken pecan meats

Mix all ingredients together and shape into half moons. Place on a cookie sheet. Bake at 275°. Cool slightly. Roll in powdered sugar while still warm.

PEANUT BUTTER COOKIES
(the recipe of Mrs. Frank Hodges who is 100 years old)

1/2 cup granulated sugar
1/2 cup brown sugar
1/3 cup peanut butter
1/2 cup shortening
1 egg

Cream all the above ingredients in order given, and add:

1 1/2 cup flour
1 tsp. baking soda
1/2 tsp. salt
1/2 tsp. vanilla

Roll in balls and let chill. Place on cookie sheet and press with a fork. Bake at 325° for about 10 minutes.

SUGAR COOKIES
in memory of Jewel Mitchell

1 cup sugar
2 sticks oleo margarine
1 egg
1 tsp. vanilla
2 1/2 cups flour
1/2 tsp. baking soda

Mix ingredients together and chill for about 15 minutes. Then roll into walnut size balls and mash down twice with a glass that has been dipped in sugar. Do this after putting the cookies in baking pan. Bake at 350° for about 10 minutes.

MARIE MILLS' STAINED GLASS COOKIES
a Holiday Treat

1/2 cup oleo margarine
2 eggs
1 large package (12 oz.) chocolate chips

Cook in double boiler until thick. Cool and then add:

1 large package small marshmallows
 (colored)
2 cups pecans

Shape into roll and roll in powdered sugar. Chill well and slice.

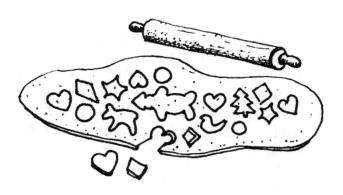

My Aunt Jane's cream puffs were taken to Sunday dinner-on-the-grounds in Ft. Sumner, New Mexico.

CREAM PUFFS
in memory of Aunt Jane Rogers
circa 1930

1 cup flour
1/2 cup butter
4 eggs (unbeaten)
1 cup boiling water

Grease a baking sheet 15 1/2 x 11 inches. Start oven 10 minutes before ready to bake at 450°.

Put butter in 3 quart saucepan. Pour boiling water over butter, heat just to boiling point, stirring until butter melts. Sift flour, measure and add all at once to butter mixture. Stir constantly with wooden spoon until mixture leaves side of pan and forms a ball. Remove from heat. Immediately add eggs one at a time, beating to a smooth paste after each. Then beat mixture until smooth and velvety. Drop by heaping Tbsp. onto a baking sheet, keeping about 3 inches apart. Form puffs round and high in center. Bake 15 minutes or until well puffed and delicate. Then reduce heat to 300° and bake for 30 or 40 minutes. This cooks the centers thoroughly, but puffs become no browner. Makes 12-14 puffs. Remove to cake rack to cool.

Cut off tops with sharp knife and fill with your favorite cream filling (chocolate, lemon or butterscotch), sweetened fruit or ice cream. Hot creamed chicken is good. Try it. After you have cut the tops off and before filling the puffs, pull out a little inside of puff so it will hold more filling. Serve as soon as possible after filled.

The first candy was made by physicians long after the landing of the Pilgrims to cover up the bad taste of medicine. This is how the sugar-coated pill evolved. Unmedicated candy wasn't made until after the days of our first president.

TIPS FOR MAKING CANDY

1. Cook candy in heavy saucepan large enough to allow to boil. A 2 quart pan will usually be right. Caramels require a 3 quart size.

2. Cook creamy candies rapidly and stir frequently until sugar is dissolved. Reduce heat and cook slowly without stirring.

3. Keep scraping down sugar crystals from the side of pan with tip of spoon or cheesecloth wrapped on tines of a fork dipped in cold water.

4. A candy thermometer is helpful but should not be depended on alone because of the change in atmospheric pressure. It's recommended that you use both thermometer and cold test.

5. Make the cold water test by removing pan of candy from fire. Fill a cup with cold water. Allow candy to fall in small drops rather than large ones into water. If a drop can be formed into a ball that will hold its shape, the candy is done. If not, continue to cook.

6. Cool creamy candies before beginning to beat. This will prevent sugaring.

7. A wooden spoon is best for stirring.

8. Do not put hot candy in a cold place. Let it cool at room temperature. Do not stir or shake pan.

Horehound is a bitter plant from the mint family. The bitter juice extracted from its white, downy leaves was used to make cough medicine or candy. Horehound candy was made by my grandmother when she came to visit us every summer. We would gather the horehound from our pasture.

She traveled by train, and her only luggage was a trunk that had a tray in the top. Her trunk and its contents were really fascinating to us.

HOREHOUND CANDY

Boil horehound in a little water until the juice is extracted. Strain through a cheesecloth. Boil any desired quantity of sugar with just enough water to dissolve the sugar. Stir in the juice. Work the sugar with a spoon against the sides of the pan until it grows thick and creamy. Pour in a buttered pan. When nearly cold, mark in squares and let dry.

This recipe was used around the turn of the century for teenage taffy pull parties.

PULLED TAFFY
circa 1900

Either sugar or molasses taffy may be pulled. For sugar taffy, boil together to the soft ball stage 3 cupfuls of sugar, 1/2 cupful of vinegar, 1/2 cupful of water. Now add 1 lump of butter, stirred in quickly, and boil until it hardens and becomes brittle in cold water. Add desired flavor just before removing from fire. Pour on a buttered platter to cool. Turn in the edges as fast as it cools. When cold enough to handle, pull until it's white and brittle.

TO PULL TAFFY

The best way to pull candy is to grease the hands thoroughly with butter to prevent sticking, or the hands may be covered with flour. The work should begin as soon as the candy is cool enough to handle by hand. Work with the tips of the fingers until it grows cool. Continue to pull until it is of a light golden color or white, according to the recipe. Pull either with the help of another person or over a hook. Finally, draw out in sticks on wax paper, or other smooth surface, which may be dusted with flour and cut with shears into sticks.

I made this candy for gifts during The Great Depression.

DATE LOAF CANDY

(7 oz.) package pitted dates (chopped)
1 cup pecans (broken)
2 cups sugar
1 cup water
1 tsp. vanilla

Stir sugar and water together over low heat until the mixture is dissolved. Increase heat and boil until forms soft ball in cold water. Add dates and cook for 5 minutes. Do not have fire hot, because it can burn ingredients. Remove from heat and beat thoroughly. Add vanilla and pecans. Beat until stiff enough to mold when poured in a very damp flour sack. We had flour and meal sacks just for this purpose. Butter your hands and mold the mixture into a long roll. You can add 1/2 cup of well drained pineapple to the dates. Gives a little different taste. If you use pineapple, cook a little longer. Let set overnight, and remove from cloth and slice.

CREAMY PRALINES
in memory of Nova Crow

3 cups sugar
1 cup buttermilk
1 tsp. baking soda
1/2 tsp. salt

Cook to soft boil stage when tested in cold water. Add soda and salt. Beat until color dulls. Pour into buttered platter and cut in squares.

AUNT BILL'S BROWN CANDY

6 cups sugar
2 cups cream or canned milk
1 Tbsp. white or corn syrup
1/2 cup butter or oleo
1/4 tsp. baking soda
1 tsp. vanilla
2 cups pecans (broken)

Melt 2 cups of sugar in a heavy skillet over low heat. Stir with wooden spoon as it caramelizes for about 30 minutes. This is the flavor secret of this candy. While caramelizing sugar, place 4 cups of sugar, cream and syrup in a large saucepan and bring to a boil. Add caramelized sugar to the boiling syrup. Pour it in a very thin stream, stirring constantly. After the two are mixed, continue cooking over medium heat to 242° on a candy thermometer, or until a firm ball is formed when dropped into cold water. Remove from heat, add butter (cut in small pieces) and soda. Stir only until butter melts. Cool undisturbed 20 minutes. Add vanilla and nuts, and beat until thick and creamy. Pour into greased pans and set. Yields about 4 pounds.

I've used this recipe for nearly 60 years. This fudge was made during a break when a foursome got together to play auction bridge (Now they only play contract bridge).

FUDGE

2 cups sugar
3/4 cup top milk (the cream that rose to
          top). Finish filling the cup with
          white Karo syrup. You could use
          part condensed milk to replace
          top milk
1/2 cup or less cocoa
1 tsp. vanilla
nuts (optional)

Rub butter around the rim of the skillet to keep ingredients from boiling over.

Mix sugar, milk, cocoa and syrup together. Stir until dissolved over low heat. Increase heat and do not stir again. When it forms a soft ball in a small amount in cold water, put in butter. Then set aside for about 20 minutes until cool. Add vanilla and beat until it is thickened and heavy enough to stand alone when piled up. Put in well buttered pan and cut in squares. I use a square Pyrex dish now.

Blanch Hatton made and sold pounds and pounds of peanut butter brittle at Christmas time to earn extra money.

PEANUT BUTTER BRITTLE
in memory of Blanch Hatton

Boil 2 cups sugar, 3/4 cup water and 1 cup white syrup until a soft ball forms in cold water. Add 2 cups raw peanuts. Cook until golden brown. Remove from fire, and add 1/4 tsp. salt, 1 tsp. baking soda, 1 Tbsp. butter and 1 tsp. vanilla. Pour on hard surface. Rub butter on hands and start stretching from outside as soon as cool enough to handle. Cut with scissors as you stretch. Keep stretching until off board.

AN EVENING PRAYER
by Charles H. Gabriel

If I have wounded any soul today,
If I have cause one foot to go astray,
If I have walked in my own wilful way,
Dear Lord, forgive!

If I have uttered idle words or vain,
If I have turned aside from want or pain,
Lest I myself shall suffer thru the strain,
Dear Lord, forgive!

Forgive the sins I have confessed to Thee;
Forgive the secret sins I do not see;
O guide me, love me, and my Keeper be,
In Jesus' name.

"A brother offended is harder to be won than a strong city;
and their contentions are like the bars of a castle."
Proverbs 18:19

BREADS

"Baking day" isn't on the housewife's calendar anymore. Fresh everyday at the bakery or grocery is a profusion of breads, rolls, cakes and pastries. Also, you can buy any kind of bakery mix needed.

MAKING BREAD IN YESTERDAY YEARS
Excerpts from a book of household hints printed in 1909

MAKING BREADS

You want to use the best flour possible. You can apply 3 tests to tell if flour will make good bread. First, it should be of creamy color. Second, it will cake slightly when gathered up into hand, falling apart and will feel sorta gritty between fingers. Third, the wetting capacity is different from poor flour. One quart of first class bread flour will absorb 1 1/2 cupfuls of water. Before buying a barrel or even 1/2 barrel of flour, buy a bagful, try 1 sort after another, use the same yeast and the same care with the mixing, raising and baking. Soon you will discover the flour you will have the best success with, then stick to that brand. As far as yeast none is better than the compressed yeast which you can find in the smallest village for the cost of 2 cents.

The molding cloth is better than a molding board to work with the dough. It holds more flour, and soft dough will not stick. As the flour works in the dough sift in more flour, rubbing it in the cloth with your hand. It can be used a number of times before being washed. When it goes to laundry, soak it for one hour in cold water and rinse several times before putting it in hot suds. Hot water would turn the flour into dough. Then it would be no easy task to get clean.

Sift in a pan 4 or 5 quarts of flour and set it over the resorivore or in a very moderate oven to warm. Cold flour always retard the action of the yeast. Scald 1 pint of cold milk and pour into your breadpan over 2 tsp. salt. Add 1 pint of cold water, then 1 yeast cake dissolved in 1/2 cup of lukewarm water. To this liquid add 7 to 8 cupfuls of warm flour and beat batter thoroughly. Do not stop beating until is a mass of bubbles. Then add more flour until you have a soft dough. Now, it is ready to knead. You work the dough to the center, pressing it away with the palms, gently yet quickly. As you work you can see how the air is doing its duty, for the dough becomes full of little bubbles and blisters. When it is smooth as satin, elastic and does not stick and is real spongey, it will rise quickly. It's now ready to set to rise. Wash the bread pan and grease well and even the lid you cover it with. This makes the dough slip out easy after the next raising. Put on the cover and set the pan in a warm place. When it has doubled in bulk, drop it again on the molding cloth and shape into loaves. The second kneading is a slight one, only enough to prepare it for the pans and get rid of any large bubbles which if left would mean holes in the bread. Have the pans greased, using a butter brush which penetrates to every corner. Generally, you will want each pan half full of dough.

After bread is in pan we then have to find a place for them to rise. In the summer I set it in the window, which of course, is closed, for a draught on rising bread hurts it. In the winter the bread goes on a shelf close to the chimney behind the stove. The shelf is covered with white oil cloth and is just wide enough for 4 loaves of bread. When set to rise, the loaves are covered with clothes made from old table linens. These are kept laundered and never used except on baking days. When it is allowed to double in bulk, pop it in a hot oven.

The hot oven should register 300°. You may go by this test: Sprinkle a tsp. of flour in bottom of oven, if it browns in 5 minutes the oven temperature is just right. If it goes chestnut brown in that treatment it's too hot and will crust too quickly. Cool the oven by putting a pan of cold water in oven, when loaves are, watch them. If you see one throwing up an awkward ridge or lump anywhere you may know the oven is too hot, and the bread is rising faster than it should. Let the oven go moderately, usually it will take about 1 hour to make the well browned loaves. Turn them out of pans immediately, brush over the crust with a butter brush and set them to cool on a wire stand. If loaves are set flat, the bottom will become moist; if they are wrapped in a cloth, there is a soft steamy crust. In the summer if the steam is not allowed to evaporate from the bread, there is danger of molding, so to must never be put away until perfectly cool.   The best place to store it is in a small shelved closet in Japaned ware, with a door that closes tight. This is better and hardier receptable than the wooden tub or stone jar that is good in some households. Never keep bread in a cellar, it is a horrible, unwholesome custom.

It is best to have your fire is such condition that it will need no replenishing while bread making is in progress.

If you don't have a wire stand for cooling bread, simply turn up a couple of bread tins and stand loaves against their edges. The idea is to let steam escape, so that your bread will neither be heavy nor moist.

Flour is almost as sensitive to odors as milk, therefore it should be kept in a perfectly clean, wholesome place. Always raise the barrel off the floor either on two strips of wood, or one of the conveyances which will swing it out and into a cupboard. Never use flour for anything without sifting first. It may not be perfectly clean from any foreign object.

HOMINY FRITTERS
circa 1914

2 level cupfuls cold cooked hominy
2 eggs
1/2 cupful milk
1 level tsp. salt
1 level tsp. baking powder
1 1/2 level cupfuls flour
1/2 cupful chopped cooked ham

Put hominy in bowl and add well beaten eggs, milk, salt, ham and baking powder sifted with flour. Beat thoroughly and drop by large spoonfuls in plenty of smoking hot fat.   Fry until nearly browned, then drain on paper and serve hot. Sufficient for 15 fritters.

PARKER HOUSE ROLLS

1 cup milk
5 Tbsp. sugar
1 Tbsp. salt
1 pkg. yeast
1 cup lukewarm water
6 cups sifted flour
6 Tbsp. melted shortening

Scald milk, add sugar and salt. Cool to lukewarm. Dissolve yeast in lukewarm water and add to lukewarm milk. Add 3 cups flour and beat until perfectly smooth. Add melted shortening and remaining flour or enough to make a dough that's easily handled. Knead well. Place in a greased bowl. Cover and set in warm place, free from draft. Let rise until double in bulk for about 1 1/2 hours. Roll out 3/8 inch thick and cut with a 2 1/2 inch biscuit cutter. Crease lightly through center with dull edge of knife and brush lightly with melted butter. Fold over in pocket book shape. Place close together in well greased shallow pan, cover and let rise for about 1 hour until double in bulk. Bake at 425° for about 1 hour.

KITCHEN KAPERS: To heat left-over bread, sprinkle lightly with water and place in a paper sack. Roll the end and tightly close with paper clips. Heat in 400° oven until crust is crisp and piping hot. Just like freshly baked bread.

REFRIGERATOR ROLLS

Follow directions for Parker House Rolls. When double in bulk, punch dough down in bowl. Brush lightly with melted shortening. Cover well and place in refrigerator until needed. To use, cut off as much dough as desired. Punch dough down. Shape into rolls and place in well greased pan. Cover and let rise in warm place free from draft until double in bulk. Bake in hot oven at 425° for 15 to 20 minutes. This dough will keep 4 to 5 days in refrigerator and bake as desired.

FEATHER DINNER ROLLS

2 pkgs. dry yeast
1/2 cup warm water
1/3 cup + 1 Tbsp. sugar
1 cup milk (scalded and cool)
1/3 cup oil
1 tsp. salt
2 eggs (beaten)
4 cups flour

Dissolve yeast in warm water with 1 Tbsp. sugar. When milk has cooled, add all ingredients except flour. Beat well, gradually add 4 cups flour to make soft dough. Let rise until double in bulk. Knead for about 10 minutes. Make into rolls or refrigerate. Bake at 350° for 20 to 30 minutes.

Georgia Williams (Mrs. Luck Williams) found this recipe in the "Oklahoma Farmer Stockman" and gave it to me in the 1950's. Mrs. Williams was in her 80's, badly crippled with rheumatoid arthritis and in a wheelchair. She said, "My man will now have hot biscuits every morning as long as I'm able."

ANGEL BISCUITS

5 cups flour (unsifted)
1/4 cup sugar
3 tsp. baking powder
1 tsp. baking soda
1 tsp. salt
1 cup shortening
1 pkg. dry yeast
2 Tbsp. warm water
2 cups buttermilk

Sift dry ingredients together. Cut in shortening. Dissolve yeast in warm water and add with buttermilk to dry ingredients. Mix well. Turn out on a lightly floured board and add more flour if necessary, roll to 1/2 inch thickness. Cut and then dip in melted butter or fold to make in pocketbook rolls. You can stack several together and brush on butter in between layers on a greased cookie sheet. Bake at 400° for 15 minutes. This will refrigerate for days. Pinch off dough as needed.

BAKING POWDER BISCUITS

2 cups all purpose flour
2 1/2 to 3 tsp. baking powder
1 tsp. salt
1/3 cup shortening (less if using lard)
about 3/4 cup milk

Measure sifted flour, add baking powder and salt. Cut in cold shortening with pastry blender. Stir in with fork enough milk to make soft dough, being sure that all flour disappears. Turn out on board, knead gently. Pat dough 1/2 inch thick and cut. Bake at 450° for 12 to 15 minutes.

RED EYE GRAVY

Leave the fat in skillet where you have pan broiled ham. Remove ham and heat fat until really hot, but not smoking. Stir up all the crusty particles. Pour the hot fat in a bowl and quickly add 1 /2 cups boiling water to the pan. Let it boil up once. Add the hot fat and put in a gravy boat. Sop with hot biscuits.

STICKY CINNAMON BUNS
in memory of Bernice Roach

1 package yeast roll mix or your own recipe. Mix and set aside to rise. Mix 1/2 cup dark Karo syrup, 2 Tbsp. melted margarine and 1/4 cup brown sugar in a large iron skillet. When dough has risen, roll into rectangles 1/8 inch thick. Spread with a mixture of margarine, sugar and cinnamon. Roll up like a jelly roll, cut into slices, put the cut side up in skillet, cover and let rise until double in bulk. Bake at 375° for 30 to 40 minutes. When done turn pan upside down over plate. Let set a few minutes. Shake to remove the rolls. Slightly warm the mixture in the skillet before putting the rolls in for the second rise. They will rise quickly.

ONION BATTER BREAD

1 Tbsp. oleo margarine
1 egg
3 Tbsp. onions (minced)
3/4 cup corn meal (yellow)
1/4 tsp. baking soda
1/2 tsp. salt
1 1/2 cup buttermilk

Put 1 Tbsp. of oleo margarine in 1 quart casserole dish in 400° oven to melt while preparing batter. Beat 1 egg and add remaining ingredients and heat until smooth. Turn into casserole dish and bake for 30 to 35 minutes until center is barely set. To serve, spoon from casserole dish and pass the butter.

MARVIN ALLEN'S DILL BREAD

1 cup cottage cheese
2 Tbsp. shortening
1 egg
1 tsp. salt
2 tsp. dill seed
1 tsp. onion flakes
1 Tbsp. shortening or use liquid oil
2 1/2 cups all purpose flour
1 pkg. dry yeast
1/4 tsp. baking soda
1/2 warm water

Heat slightly the cottage cheese. Stir in sugar, oil, salt, 1 egg, onion, dill seed, and baking soda. Add yeast that has been mixed with warm water. Add flour. Knead for about 10 minutes and let rise until double in bulk. Punch down and let rise again. Bake in greased loaf pan at 350° for 1 hour.

Real southern corn bread has no flour and no sugar. It is only made with yellow corn meal, with a thin batter, and baked with a golden brown crust.

REALLY SOUTHERN CORN BREAD

1 egg
2 cups buttermilk
2 cups corn meal (yellow)
1 tsp. salt
1 tsp. baking soda
4 Tbsp. butter or bacon fat

Beat the egg and add to buttermilk, sift dry ingredients to liquid. Stir in melted butter quickly. Turn in a well greased baking pan 8 x 10 inches that is sizzling hot. Bake at 400° for 30 minutes.

JALAPENO CORN BREAD

3 cups corn bread mix
1/2 cup salad oil
1 large onion (grated)
1 small can cream style corn
1/2 cup grated cheese
1/4 lb. bacon (fried and crumbled)
2 1/2 cups milk
3 eggs
2 Tbsp. sugar (I leave out)
1/2 cup jalapeno peppers (I use less)

Combine ingredients and bake. I heat about 3 Tbsp. bacon drippings in an iron skillet and then pour contents in skillet. Bake at 400° for 30 minutes.

CORN BREAD
Jean Boyd

1 cup corn meal
2 Tbsp. wheat germ
2 Tbsp. flour
1 egg
1 cup buttermilk
1 tsp. salt
2 tsp. baking powder
1/4 tsp. baking soda

Mix ingredients. Grease and flour pan.
Bake 450° for 15 to 20 minutes.

Corn meal mush was made for supper. If we had any mush left over, it was molded in a dish, fried and served for breakfast.

CORN MEAL MUSH

5 cups water
1 1/2 tsp. salt
1 cup cornmeal

Add slowly (sifted slowly would be easier) 1 cup corn meal with 1 1/2 tsp. salt. Reduce heat and cook until thick for about 15 to 20 minutes, stirring frequently. Serve hot with butter.

FRIED MUSH FOR BREAKFAST

Put the left over mush in loaf pan. Slice into 1/4 to 1/2 inch slices. Dip slices in meal and fry in heavy skillet with 3 to 4 Tbsp. of oil. Serve hot with butter, if desired.

SALADS

AND SOUPS

The first mayonnaise I can remember was introduced by a Wesson Oil representative that did "in house" demonstrations, not in the grocery store. She had all the ingredients and equipment with her, which included a rotary beater with a lid made into it, so that it would fit on a crock that had "Wesson Oil" printed on the side. I have the crock. If anyone has the beater and lid combination, I would be interested in buying it. The bottom of the Wesson Oil crock was rounded so the beater would fit better. She served the mayonnaise mixed with a relish between soda crackers. To us it was just plain old "chow chow." After this demonstration my mother began to make slaw.

MAYONNAISE
circa 1925

Mix sugar, dry mustard and salt with half of vinegar. Continue beating with a rotary beater, add the oil and rest of the vinegar alternately. As soon as oil is added, it begins to thicken instantly. Continue beating until thick and fluffy. Add celery seed last. Serve on any tossed green salad.

MRS. MILLS' PET MILK MAYONNAISE

1 tsp. salt
1/2 tsp. paprika
1 tsp. sugar
1 1/4 tsp. mustard
1/4 cup Pet milk
1/4 cup olive oil
1 Tbsp. lemon juice
1 Tbsp. vinegar
cayenne pepper (a small dash)

Mix salt, paprika, sugar, mustard, cayenne pepper and milk together. Add oil drop by drop until mixture thickens a little. Mix lemon juice and vinegar. Add, alternating with the oil, 1 tsp. at a time until oil is used, beating thoroughly after each addition. Ingredients should be very cold while mixing. Set the bowl in ice water. Keep in bowl in ice water until ready to serve.

I have used this recipe since World War II. You can double or triple the dressing recipe. Refrigerate for use when needed.

COLE SLAW
in memory of Wella Ligon

1 cabbage 2 lbs. (cut fine)
1 cup salad dressing
1/2 cup sugar
1/4 cup vinegar

Mix well and put over cabbage. Keeps well and is easily made.

WALDORF SALAD
an old recipe

2 cups apples (chopped)
1 cup nuts (chopped or broken)
1 cup celery (diced)

Mix with preferred dressing. Serve on lettuce leaf. You could add 1 cup shredded cabbage. To me the cabbage enhances the taste of the salad.

24 HOUR CABBAGE SLAW

1 large head of cabbage
2 large onions (sliced in rings)
3/4 cup sugar
1 cup vinegar
1 tsp. celery salt
1 tsp. sugar
1 Tbsp. prepared mustard
1 1/2 tsp. salt
1 cup Wesson Oil

Shred cabbage - a blender works really well. Slice onions and separate in rings. Place layers of cabbage and onion in large bowl using all. Sprinkle sugar over this, lifting with fork to allow sugar to go to bottom. Mix vinegar, salt and 1 Tbsp. of sugar, mustard and celery salt. Let this come to a boil. Add oil, then add to cabbage while mixture is hot. Refrigerate for 24 hours. Good for outdoor cookouts. Will keep indefinitely, if you hide it.

MRS. MILLS' SALAD VEGETABLES
from her book of pasted recipes

celery
lettuce
cucumbers
onions
radishes

To prepare the uncooked vegetables for salad, pick over, discard bruised portions, look out for insects by washing each leaf or stalk separately. Drain and pile in order on a wet towel. Lay vegetables on ice or where they will be cold. They will keep by this method for several days. Do not scrape celery until ready for table. Pare cucumbers slices, slice onions and put in a bowl covered with vinegar and a little sugar. Serve separately. Arrange lettuce in deep bowl, large dark leaves on outside and so on with the light color and small ones in the center, as if half opened.

Celery looks best in large upright glass with its delicate tips opening out like a flower. The radishes may be served in the center of the lettuce leaves. Put out French dressing and each person may dress the salad vegetables to his own liking.

5 CUP SALAD
in memory of Christine Rogers (my sister-in-law)

1 cup mandarin oranges
1 cup pineapple (drained)
1 cup coconut
1 cup marshmallows (miniature)
1 cup sour cream

Mix in order given. Chill and add cream before serving.

WILTED LETTUCE SALAD
in memory of Leslie Hickman

Select very fresh spring lettuce leaves. Wash carefully and chop 6 cups of leaves. Add 4 finely chopped young onions with tops and toss mixture lightly. Fry 6 slices of bacon and drain. In the hot bacon dripping, add 1/2 to 1 tsp. salt, 1 tsp. sugar and 2 Tbsp. vinegar. Stir well, heat and pour immediately over lettuce, toss lightly to coat all leaves. Crumble cooked bacon over top. Chopped hard-cooked eggs could be added to make it more nutritious. Serves 4 to 6.

I have used this recipe since World War II.

CRANBERRY SALAD
Yada Corbin

2 cups cranberries
3 cups sugar (I use 1 cup)
1 cup water
1 cup miniature marshmallows
1 cup apples (diced)
1 cup celery (chopped)
1 cup pecans (chopped)
3 small packages Strawberry Jell-o
1 cup boiling water

Cook together, cranberries, sugar and 1 cup water until cranberries pop. Add marshmallows and blend. Let cool and add apples, celery and nuts. Add the one cup boiling water to the Jell-o in a large bowl. When cool, add all ingredients to Jell-o and refrigerate overnight. A must for Christmas and Thanksgiving dinner.

The first Jell-o I can remember was served to us when we went to visit the Kellers -- new friends who lived about 35 miles away. We left early in the morning for our visit and left early to get back home to do the chores before dark. I couldn't tell you anything else Mrs. Keller served that day in 1923, but that plain, red Jell-o with whipped cream was so pretty.

These are current recipes given to me by Olevia Robinson. Congealed salads are her specialty. Don't be afraid to try all of them; they are really good.

HOLIDAY SALAD
Olevia Robinson

1 small box strawberry Jell-o
2 1/2 cups water (boiling)
1 can whole cranberry sauce
1 small box lemon Jell-o
1 package (8 oz.) cream cheese
1 small can pineapple (crushed with
    juice)
1 cup nuts (chopped)

Dissolve strawberry Jell-o in 1 1/4 cup boiling water, add cranberry sauce and mix well. Chill until partially set. Pour into mold and chill until firm. Dissolve lemon Jell-o in remaining water (1 1/4 cup), add cream cheese, beat until smooth, add pineapple. Chill until partially set, stir in nuts. Pour over cranberry mixture. Chill until firm. Serves 12.

KITCHEN KAPERS: For a real good Thousand Island dressing, mix 1 cup salad dressing and 1 cup ketchup. Bob Mills

CONGEALED SUNSHINE SALAD
Olevia Robinson

2 packages (3 oz. each) orange Jell-o
1 package (8 oz.) cream cheese
     (softened)
1/8 tsp. salt
2 cups water (boiling)
1 can (no. 2) crushed pineapple
     (drained and syrup reserved)
1 can (11 oz.) mandarin oranges
     (chopped and drained with syrup
     reserved)
1/2 cup pecans (chopped)

Blend Jell-o, cream cheese and salt. Stir in boiling water until mixture dissolves. Add reserved juices and mix well. Chill until mixture begins to thicken, fold in pineapple, orange sections and pecans. Pour in large mold or 12 small molds. Refrigerate until congealed.

THREE LAYER FRUIT SALAD
Olevia Robinson

2 packages (3 oz. each) orange Jell-o
2 cups water (boiling)
1 can (small) frozen orange juice
     concentrate
1 can (large) pineapple (crushed)
2 packages (small) instant lemon
     pudding mix
2 cans (small) mandarin orange
     segments
2 cups milk (cold)
whipped topping

Dissolve Jell-o in boiling water, stir in orange juice and fruits. Pour into large flat pan, refrigerate until firm. Prepare lemon pudding mix with milk, according to package directions. Spread over Jell-o mixture. Refrigerate until ready to serve. Spread with whipped topping. Serves 15.

MOLDED CRANBERRY RELISH SALAD
Olevia Robinson

1 package (3 oz.)strawberry Jell-o
1 cup water (boiling)
1 jar (14 oz.)cranberry orange relish
1 Tbsp. lemon juice
1/8 tsp. salt
1 can (15 oz.) crushed pineapple
        (drained and reserved)
1 package (3 oz.) lemon Jell-o
2 cups marshmallows (miniature)
cream cheese (3 oz.)
1/2 cup sour cream
1/2 cup nuts (chopped)
1/2 cup heavy cream (whipped)

Dissolve strawberry Jell-o in boiling water, add relish, lemon juice and salt. Pour into 6 cup mold or individual molds. Chill until firm. Combine reserved juice and enough water to make 1 1/2 cups, heat. Dissolve lemon Jell-o in hot juice. Add marshmallows, stir to dissolve. May have to place over heat, blend cream cheese and sour cream with egg beater. Add sour cream mixture and nuts to marshmallow mixture. Cool. Fold in whipped cream and pour on top of relish mixture. Chill.

KRAUT SALAD
in memory of Maude Ellington

1 cup sugar
1/2 cup vinegar
1 tsp. mustard seed
1 tsp. celery seed
1 can kraut (well drained)
1/4 cup Wesson Oil
1/2 cup celery (chopped)
1/2 cup onions (chopped)
1/2 cup green peppers (chopped)
1 large jar pimento (chopped)

Bring to boil sugar, vinegar, mustard seed and celery seed. Set aside. Mix kraut, oil, celery, onion, green peppers and pimento. Pour oil over kraut, then add rest of ingredients. Store in covered bowl and refrigerate.

CAULIFLOWER SALAD

1 head cauliflower (chopped)
1 tomato (chopped)
1 onion (chopped)
1 cup cheese (grated)
1 carrot (grated)
1 Tbsp. sugar
mayonnaise (enough to moisten)
salt and pepper to taste

Combine all ingredients and refrigerate 6 hours before serving.

THE BEST POTATO SALAD

Lois Southall - high school classmate

4 large potatoes (cooked and cubed)
1/2 cup onion (chopped)
1/2 cup celery (chopped) or
     1 tsp. celery seed
4 hard cooked eggs (diced)
1/2 cup dill or sweet pickles (diced)

Put potatoes in large bowl, and rest of ingredients in order given. Pour dressing over potato salad and mix. Chill for several hours before serving.

DRESSING FOR POTATO SALAD

1/2 cup sugar
1/2 cup vinegar
1/2 cup water

Bring to boil and pour slowly over 2 beaten eggs. Pour back in pan and cook until thickened.

Marvin and Thelma Allen

This salad was brought to my house when my father died in 1953. I mentioned to Mrs. Mabry how good it was and she said, "Oh! That's Grandma Murray's recipe" (Myrtle Thomas' mother). She said it was brought to "dinner on the ground" many times. Mrs. Murray was a charter member of Elm and Hudson Street Church of Christ where I have attended for 60 years. I was always expected to bring this rice salad to every Allen family get-together.

RICE SALAD
circa mid-20's

2 cups cooked rice (cooled)
1 can (16 oz.) crushed pineapple. Use juice
18 marshmallow (cut with scissors dipped in water. Today you would use 2 cups miniature marshmallows)
1 cup whipping cream

Let pineapple set overnight with marshmallows. Add the rice the next morning. Add whipped cream just before serving. A must for Christmas, Thanksgiving and anytime in between. Use for a dessert or with meat.

HOT CHICKEN SALAD

4 cups chicken (cooked)
4 eggs (hard cooked and sliced)
2 cups celery
1 large jar pimento
2 Tbsp. onions (minced)
3/4 cup Miracle Whip
2 Tbsp. lemon juice
1 tsp. salt
1 1/2 cups potato chips (crushed)
1 cup cheese (grated)
2/3 cup toasted almonds (chopped)

Combine all but last 3 ingredients. Place in large rectangular dish. Let stand in refrigerator overnight. Before cooking, top with potato chips, almonds and cheese. Bake at 400° for 20 to 25 minutes and serve.

CABBAGE PATCH STEW

Make 1 lb. pork sausage in balls (walnut size) and steam with enough water to barely cover. Cook while preparing next 3 ingredients. Add 1 cup diced onions, 1 cup celery and 1/2 cup bell peppers. Let steam for about 10 minutes and add 1 can whole kernel corn. Add 2 cups grated cabbage and 1 can tomatoes with juice. If I use whole tomatoes, I chop in can. Add salt and chili powder to taste. I cook down fairly low. But if you want it thin, add more water. Great with corn bread.

CROCK POT STEW

2 lbs. stew meat
3 to 4 potatoes
3 carrots (sliced)
1 package onion soup mix
2 to 3 cups water
1 can peas
a dash of dill seed
2 to 3 bay leaves

Cook all together in crock pot. Last 15 minutes, add peas. The last 5 to 10 minutes, add paste made from 2 to 3 cups water, salt, pepper, dash of dill seed, and bay leaves. Cook on low heat for about 6 hours.

TEXAS STEW

1 lb. ground beef
1 cup celery (chopped)
1/2 cup onion (chopped)
1/2 cup green peppers (chopped)
1 can (10 oz.) Rotel tomatoes
2 small cans minestrone soup
1 can ranch-style beans
2 cans water (use bean can)

Brown beef. Take chopped onions, chopped green peppers, chopped celery and steam in meat for a few minutes until tender. Add 10 oz. can of tomatoes, 2 small cans of minestrone soup, beans, and 2 cans of water. Simmer for 30 minutes. For a milder stew, use 1/2 of the Rotel tomatoes.

POOR MAN'S STEW

6 medium potatoes (cubed)
2 lbs. chunk bologna (cubed)
1 can (16 oz.) mixed peas and carrots
1 can biscuits

Cook potatoes until done. Add peas and carrots and bologna. Heat to a boil. Pour into a casserole. Top with biscuits. Bake at 475° until brown.

KITCHEN KAPERS: A dash of curry powder is good in soups.

MARVIN ALLEN'S STEW

1 1/2 to 2 lbs. ground beef (lean)

Saute` beef in heavy skillet until pink color is barely gone.

In the meantime, cook in a large pot until nearly done these ingredients (use plenty of water):

5 potatoes
1 large onion
4 to 6 carrots (sliced)
4 to 6 stalks celery (diced)
1 can tomatoes

Add meat, 3 to 4 dashes of Tabasco sauce, 4 tsp. Worchestershire sauce, salt and pepper to taste, and chili powder if desired. Simmer for about 30 minutes. If thinner than you like, thicken with 1/2 cup rice (raw) and cook a little longer or thicken with instant potatoes. Paprika gives it a nice color. Serve with fresh corn bread.

MARIE MILLS' CHICKEN SOUP

Boil 1 large broiler chicken until tender with plenty of water for broth. Cool and debone. Chicken chunks are preferred. Cook together in chicken broth 3/4 cup rice, 3 to 4 grated carrots, 1 large onion diced, and 3 to 4 stalks of chopped celery. Cook until nearly tender. Then add chopped chicken and simmer about 30 minutes. Add 2 packages of Lipton's Cup of Soup (optional). Salt and pepper to taste.

POTATO SOUP

3 to 4 baking potatoes
2 stalks celery (finely chopped)
1 medium onion (finely diced)
2 to 3 Tbsp. butter
1 can evaporated milk
salt and pepper to taste

Simmer first 3 ingredients listed with about 2 to 3 Tbsp. butter and enough water to cover. When potatoes are tender, add 1 small can evaporated milk. Add salt and pepper to taste. If you want a thicker soup, take out part of potatoes and mash. Put back into soup and simmer about 5 minutes longer. Add more milk if desired.

GEORGIA STEAK STEW
Jack Campbell

Melt 1 stick oleo and whip in 1 cup flour to make a smooth paste. Stir in 2 quarts water. Saute` 2 cups ground beef (chuck), drain off excess grease and add to soup. Add 1 cup each onions, carrots and celery, which have been cubed and par boiled. Add 2 cups frozen mixed vegetables, 1 can tomatoes, 1 Tbsp. Accent, and 2 Tbsp. beef concentrate (granules or cubes), and 1 tsp. black pepper. Bring to a boil, reduce to simmer and cook until vegetables are tender. May be frozen.

MRS. MILLS' CREAM OF TOMATO SOUP
circa 1910

1 quart milk
1 pint canned or stewed tomatoes
3 Tbsp. butter
1 bay leaf
a sprig of parsley
blade of mace
1 tsp. sugar
1/4 tsp. baking soda
2 Tbsp. flour

Put the tomatoes on to stew with the bay leaf, parsley and mace. Let them stew 15 minutes. Put the milk on to boil in a farina boiler. Rub butter and flour together, add to the milk when boiling and stir constantly until thickens. Now press the tomatoes through a sieve, and if ready to serve, add the sugar and soda at once. It must not go on the fire after mixing the milk with tomatoes, or it will separate. If you are not ready to serve, let them stand on fire and mix when ready to serve.

CREAM OF BROCCOLI SOUP
delicious and easy

Cook these ingredients slowly in a small amount of water:

2 cups broccoli (frozen)
1 cup celery (chopped real fine)
1 cup onion(chopped)

Add to:

1 can cream of broccoli soup
1 can celery soup
1 can cream of chicken soup
3 cans milk
1 - 3 cans water

Mix and heat thoroughly. While hot add 1/4 to 1/2 lbs. of Velveeta cheese. Let simmer a few minutes and serve with a good cracker or corn bread. You will not need salt, because the soup and cheese are salty. You can add more black pepper.

KITCHEN KAPERS: If dry beans are not cooking tender or going to be "hard. " put in 1/4 tsp. baking powder. It will do the trick.

RELISHES

AND

PRESERVES

This recipe was very popular during The Depression. It was easy and economical to make. It was said that 1/3 of the vegetables used at that time were raised on the farm or in small gardens.

BREAD AND BUTTER PICKLES
in memory of Myrtle Thomas

20 to 25 cucumbers (sliced)
8 large white onions
2 large sweet peppers
1/2 cup salt
5 cups vinegar
2 Tbsp. pickling spice
1 tsp. tumeric

Wash cucumbers, slice. Chop onions and peppers. Cover with salt, let stand 3 hours. Drain and wash. Combine sugar, vinegar, spices, and tumeric. Bring to boil, add cucumbers, heat thoroughly. Bring to boil, add cucumbers, heat thoroughly. Do not boil. Pack in sterilized jars.

CRANBERRY RELISH

Peel a large orange so thinly that you do not include the white inner layer. Remove the white layer from the orange sections and break the sections into small pieces. Put 1 lb. raw cranberries and orange peel through the course grinder of a food chopper. Add the diced orange and 2 cups sugar (I use less sugar) with 3 or 4 whole cloves. Mix well and store in a crock or in jars in a cool place for at least 2 weeks. This is a real old recipe when there was very little refrigeration. Now I would say, "put in the refrigerator." Do not cook. Makes a good Christmas gift.

PICKLED PEACH PICKLES

Mix 7 cupfuls granulated sugar, 1 pint cider vinegar, and 1 pint water. Boil for 20 minutes. Add fruit and boil until tender. To each pint add 3 whole cloves, 3 small sticks of cinnamon bark (1 inch). Fill jars with peaches, cover with hot syrup and seal. May be used for pears, crab apples, pineapple, watermelon rind and apricots. Save fruit juices for seasoning a baked ham or shoulder (pork).

MRS. MILLS' RELISH
from her book of pasted recipes

3 quarts green tomatoes
1 quart sweet peppers
1 quart onions
2 small cabbage heads

Chop, measure ingredients and put in vessel to set overnight in 1 gallon of water and 1 heaping cup of salt. Next morning put in flour sack and let drain for 4 to 5 hours.

Then take:

1 quart sugar
1 cup flour
6 Tbsp. mustard
1 Tbsp. tumeric
1 1/2 quarts vinegar
1 1/2 quarts water

Mix and let come to a boil. Add chopped ingredients and boil another 20 minutes.

SEASONING SALT

Mary Loucyle Self

1 lb. plus 10 oz. box table salt
1 tsp. onion salt
2 Tbsp. celery salt
1 Tbsp. garlic salt
2 Tbsp. paprika
4 Tbsp. black pepper
4 Tbsp. white pepper
1 Tbsp. dill seed
2 Tbsp. monosodium glutamate
4 Tbsp. sugar

Mix all ingredients and store in dark place for 24 hours before using in favorite dishes.

LYE PEELING

Add 1 oz. or 1 Tbsp. of lye to each gallon of water (boiling). Immerse the pears, peaches or big tomatoes in a dripping basket or cloth bag for 10 to 20 seconds. Remove and rinse in cold water. The skins will then peel off. Much labor is saved, and you have a smooth product.

TOMATO PRESERVES

5 lbs. ripe tomatoes
5 cups brown sugar
1/2 tsp. ground cloves
3 small sticks cinnamon
1 lemon

Peel and core tomatoes, cut in pieces. Add sugar and lemon. Cut into very small thin slices. Add spices and boil slowly for 2 hours. While hot, fill jars and seal.

PLUM JELLY

Wash and cook 2 lbs. plums in 2 cups of water until the peel bursts, about 20 to 30 minutes. Let drain in colander, and to make a pretty, clear jelly, drain through a cloth. To each cup of juice add scant cup of sugar. Don't cook more than 3 cups at a time. Let the sugar dissolve and boil rapidly until fork put in jelly will flow to a single drop from the tine or 220-222°. Turn into sterilized jars and seal with paraffin. Plums can be canned and made into jelly anytime.

WATERMELON PRESERVES

Peel rind of watermelon and remove pink meat. Cut into 1 inch squares. Put into enamel container and cover with cold salt water (1/2 cup to 1 gallon). Let stand overnight. Drain, cover with fresh cold salt water, let stand overnight. Let stand overnight for the third time. Drain well. Make syrup.

SYRUP

9 cups sugar
1 pint vinegar
1 Tbsp. whole cloves
12 pieces stick cinnamon

Add ingredients and boil 15 minutes. Add watermelon, cook 20 minutes. Remove to enamel vessel. Let stand in syrup overnight. The second morning, boil for 20 minutes. Let stand overnight. The third morning, bring to a boil. Can while hot. Rind will be firm and transparent.

MRS. MILLS' STRAWBERRY PRESERVES

1 pint strawberries
2 cups sugar
2 cups water or less
    (If strawberries have a high
    content of water, little or no water
    may be needed.)

Wash berries a few at a time in a sieve, until they are free of dirt. Drain on a soft towel or any cloth that's absorbent. Pull stems. Never work with more than a quart at a time; less is better. Put berries, water and sugar in a large pan on very low heat until al l sugar is dissolved. It will help if you shake the pan once or twice. Increase heat and boil exactly 10 minutes. Set aside until the bubbles are gone. Then add 1 pint more berries, 2 more cups sugar. Return to heat until the sugar is dissolved, bring to boil and boil 10 minutes more. Skim while cooking. Don't stir. Remove from fire and let the bubbling stop. Put berries in a shallow pan and let stand for 24 hours. Put in sterilized jars. Do not reheat. Cover with paraffin and store in a cool, dark place. If you have extra syrup left, can separately. Good on cakes, puddings and ice cream.

CHOW CHOW

3 quarts cabbage
1 quart carrots
3 quarts green tomatoes
2 quarts apples (unpeeled)
1 quart onion (grounded)
6 cups sugar
6 sweet peppers (some reds)
1 hot pepper
1 large bunch of celery
1 tsp. dry mustard
1 Tbsp. salt
1 tsp. black pepper
1 tsp. ginger
1 tsp. cayenne pepper
9 cups vinegar

Cook until clear.   Put in sterilized jars
and seal.

KITCHEN KAPERS: Hard cooked eggs should
never be boiled. Place not more than 4 in enamel or
glass pan with enough lukewarm water to cover 1/2
inch above eggs. Bring to a rapid boil, remove from
heat, cover and let stand for 15 minutes. Cool quickly
and thoroughly in cold water.   This treatment will
make shells easier to remove and will keep the dark
color off rim of egg. Eggs 3 or 4 days old will peel
easier than fresh eggs.

FOOTPRINTS

One night a man had a dream. He dreamed he was walking along the beach with the Lord. Across the sky flashed scenes from his life. For each scene, he noticed two sets of footprints in the sand; one belonging to him, and the other to the Lord.

When the last scene of his life flashed before him, he looked back at the footprints in the sand. He noticed that many times along the path of his life there was only one set of footprints. He also noticed that it happened at the very lowest and saddest times in his life.

This really bothered him and he questioned the Lord about it. "Lord, you said that once I decided to follow you, you'd walk with me all the way. But I noticed that during the most troublesome times in my life, there is only one set of footprints. I don't understand why when I needed you most you would leave me."

The Lord replied, "My precious, precious child. I love you and I would never leave you. During your times of trial and suffering, when you see only one set of footprints, it was then that I carried you."

Author unknown

MEMORIES

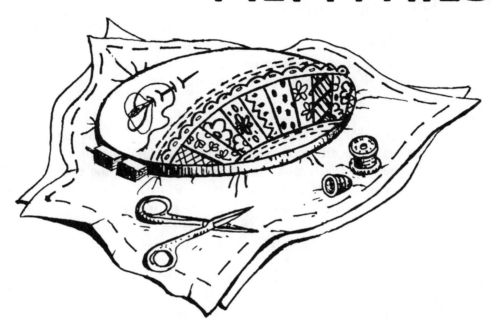

GOING TO CHURCH

We always knew we were going to Church on Sunday, because everything was planned ahead on Saturday night: Sunday clothes laid out, baths taken and shampoos done with Watkin's Shampoo. My mother prepared dinner as my father helped us dress: shoes to button, sashes to tie and dresses and underwear to button - no zippers. Only an illness would have prevented us from going to Church.

I remember going in a hack. I guess you would call it a "surrey without the fringe on top." Later, we got a car. If it rained, we had to go in the wagon or get stuck in the car (no hard surface roads) and be pulled out by a team of horses or pushed out by manpower; neither was fun. We arrived early for church in the winter time so my father could build a fire.

We met for night services by early candlelight. When returning home after church in the hack, it took 2 people to open the gate that lead to our farm; one to open the gate and one to hold the lantern. With the car, it furnished enough light to open and close the gate.

My father led the singing and did anything else there was to do. He and my brother sat on the front seat. My mother (who always wore a large brim hat), Marie and I sat a few seats back. If we were doing something we weren't supposed to, she just cut those eyes from under her hat toward us. Soon everything was under control. Somebody nearly always came home with us for Sunday dinner, if not a family, it would be a teenage boy. Usually the boys at church had their own saddle horses and would have a way home. My brother, Charlie, had his own saddle horse, Nellie, by the age of 5. My mother had her own buggy horse, May, who was the mother of Nellie.

DINNER ON THE GROUND

Every summer we would have a 2 week protracted meeting or revival. We had "dinner on the ground" both Sundays. The men would meet on the day before the meeting to build a brush arbor, put the seats from the church building under the arbor and cover the dirt floor with straw to keep down the dust.

Some of the church benches were put back-to-back to serve dinner on. A sheet was put in the bottom of a wash tub, then pulled up to wrap around the food. The sheet was later used for the table cloth. The food had to be something that wouldn't spoil, like chicken, fried on Sunday morning. Cream pies had to be cooked the same day; therefore, we had mostly cakes spread with jelly and fruit cobblers. The vegetables were what was in season, like fried okra and potatoes in a cream sauce with lots of cream and fresh butter. There were always beet pickles and potato salad, garnished so artistically with hard cooked eggs and big bowls of sliced tomatoes. "Light bread" was homemade.

MY MOTHER'S POTATO SALAD

There is no recorded recipe for my mother's potato salad - just by taste. She mashed the desired amount of potatoes, while hot, with butter and added salt and pepper to taste. She added minced onion and sour pickles chopped fine. No milk was added, because there were no refrigerators. Add dry mustard and celery seed. Add 1 part vinegar and 1/2 part of sugar in vinegar. Stir in mashed potatoes, being careful not to get too thin. Add grated eggs last. This will be a sweet/sour salad. Add more vinegar or sugar to taste. I usually add diced celery, but it was rarely found in my mother's kitchen. This is my favorite potato salad.

We always had beet pickles at Dinner on the Ground

BEET PICKLES

24 small beets
3 medium onions (sliced)
1 pint vinegar
2 Tbsp. salt
1 1/4 cup sugar
1 stick (3") cinnamon
6 whole cloves

Remove beet tops, leave roots and 1 inch stem. Put beets in saucepan, cover with boiling water and cook until beets are tender. Reserve 1 cup cooking liquid. Remove beet skins and slice. Combine the reserved liquid, vinegar, salt and sugar in kettle. Tie cinnamon and cloves in small cloth bag, place in kettle and bring to a boil. Add beets and onions. Simmer until tender. Remove spice bag. Pack beets and onions in pint jars and simmer liquid to pour over beets and onions. Fill liquid in jars within 1/2 inch of rim. Store in a dry place.

COMMUNION BREAD
made by my mother

Communion Bread is the bread taken on the first day of the week to commemorate the death, burial and resurrection of Jesus so that we can have hope of eternal life.

1 1/2 cups flour
a scant 1/2 cup lard
about 1/4 cup water

Make a well in flour. Add water and lard to well and mix with fingers, until it will make a ball. Turn on floured board and knead slightly. Divide into 2 balls. Roll into squares and score into small squares with the back of a knife. Cook about 15 minutes, until thoroughly dry, but slightly brown.

FIRST AUTOMOBILE SIGHTING

I can remember the first car I ever saw. My mother, sister and I were going somewhere in the buggy when we saw a car coming toward us. It upset my mother. She was afraid it would frighten our horse, and the horse would run away. Perhaps the driver was a salesman - the first car owners usually were. He stopped his car quite a distance from us and walked over to lead our horse safely past his car. It was a relief to my mother - our first encounter with a car.

OUR FIRST CAR

I can also remember the first car my father bought. My grandfather had bought one before we did. One of my uncles who was still at home took my father to Mineral Wells, Texas, to buy our car. My father had to have a driving lesson before he could drive it home. It was a Model T Ford Touring car. The door on the driver's side was a fake door and did not open. The driver had to crawl over that door to get to the driver's seat or enter from the right side door and slide over.

About the first tragedy I can remember involving an automobile was the accidental death of a 15 year old friend of my brother. His friend had been hunting for rabbits in his car and had started home when he saw a rabbit just over the fence on our farm. He stopped the car and grabbed his gun, probably a .22 rifle. He jumped out of the car, hung the trigger on that fake door and shot himself in the head. We lived about 1/2 mile from the scene and heard the gun fire. He died a few hours later.

Then, a few years later, a friend of our family was killed in a car accident. Accidents rarely happened back then. As a matter of fact, I can't remember the next accident. About the only accidents would be when the drivers would fail to stop when they put the car in the "car shed." They really didn't go through the car shed - the back would stop the car. That wasn't serious; they just had to repair the back of the shed. The shed was built after the purchase of the car. Our open touring car was kept in the barn for protection from the weather until the car shed could be built. Only wealthy people had closed cars that could be kept outside, but they had car sheds to protect them.

I don't remember young people racing in cars. They probably did. If my brother did, he took great pains to prevent my father from knowing it. Boys did race with horses, and my father frowned on that. That's not to say he didn't do it. My brother also did his "courtship" in a buggy.

Charlie Rogers

When my mother needed a spool of thread or something we couldn't borrow, Marie and I would saddle a horse and ride 3 miles to a little store. We borrowed baking powder and soda, salt, but not sugar. If we ran out of sugar, we just did without until we went to Mineral Wells in the car 18 miles away. There were no hard surface roads, and they could get the muddiest. Sometimes we would get stuck and everybody got out and pushed, or we had to be pulled out, not by a tractor, but by a team of horses hooked to a double tree. A lot of times we hoped for someone to drive ahead of us to make some tracks to follow in. If we planned to go somewhere the next day, we went to bed hoping it wouldn't rain or snow. There was "no going" if it did either.

There weren't any starters on those early cars, so they had to be cranked by hand. It was said that Henry Ford sent more people to hell because of the language used when the car "kicked" when being started or even broke arms. My father was never known to use a "bad word." I heard him say, "dog bite it, " a few times.

My aunt was teaching in a little country school with 2 female teachers. They were walking to town about 4 miles away. One of them got in the middle, while the other girls assisted the middle girl with her walking (playing crippled). They got a ride. I don't know how they got home. Surely they ran into some of their patrons. They didn't get the idea from Claudette Colbert's movie, "It Happened One Night." That movie was after their time.

This was said to be an old fairy tale. Whatever the source, it should be taped on the bathroom mirror.

> For all the ills under the sun,
> There is a remedy or there is none.
> If there be one, find it,
> If there be none, never mind it.

190

OUR FIRST OVERLAND TRIP

The first overland trip we made in the car was to the Ft. Worth Fatstock Show and Rodeo, a distance of 60 miles. We left early in the morning (early daylight). My mother had packed the makings for breakfast, probably in a dishpan. We stopped on the roadside, built a campfire and heated those sausages I told you about that were packed in lard. The cold biscuits were warmed in the skillet. There was also 1/2 gallon of milk in a fruit jar.

At the Livestock Show we took our first merry-go-round ride. We were turned around when we got off the ride and were ready to cry because we didn't see our parents. Just in a few seconds they came to us. Ft. Worth was the first big city we had ever seen, and the longest distance we had traveled from home. What and experience!

THE LITTLE HOUSE OUT BACK

Occasionally, my mother's younger sisters (who were away in college) would bring us paper dolls. My sister and I were allowed to use the color pages from the mail order catalogs for paper dolls, but most of the time, the Sears, Roebuck and Co. and Montgomery Ward catalogs went to the little house (privy) at the end of the trail.

That little house wasn't very popular on cold winter nights. We would take the centerfold from the Dallas semi-weekly newspaper and make a circle as large as the paper would allow, then we would cut a center circle to cover the privy hole. When finished, we held it next to the heater to warm it, then we put it under our arms to keep it warm and made a high dive to the toilet (as we called it most of the time). The heated newspaper made our trip a little more comfortable, and it didn't take long on those cold nights to get back to the big house, either.

We've had lots of improvements since those days that have made life more pleasant, but none that had the impact on our lives as the indoor toilet. When renting a house in town, the first question asked was, "Is it modern?" When have you heard that statement about a house?

191

GATHERING EGGS

Going barefoot in the springtime was lots of fun; the ground had to be warm before we were allowed to go barefoot. The cold ground was thought to give you a bad cold. We learned at an early age not to go into the chicken yard without shoes, because you wanted to avoid that "stuff" that got between your toes. You had to wash your feet, immediately, if you didn't watch your step.

Marie and I gathered the eggs in late afternoon. It was fun, except when we had to get them from under and old "settin' hen." She would peck at us when we reached under her wings to get the eggs. We took care of that problem; one would hold her head down with a broomstick, while the other would reach for the eggs.

Then there was another problem - bull or chicken snakes that would get in the nest and eat the eggs. You could count the eggs they swallowed when they wrapped themselves around a post or a tree to break the eggs. Sometimes they would swallow the nest eggs. They were made of china and were put in the nest to entice the setting hen to lay in that nest. When the snake would break the china egg, the egg would kill the snake. It was o.k. by us.

HOMEMADE LYE

My grandmother, who was born in Tennessee in 1861, told me about making lye from ashes. I never learned the details, but my 94 year old friend, Mary Loucyle Self. filled me in.

A homemade hopper was made that would hold about 5 gallons of clean ashes with a hole for drainage in the bottom. It was filled with water. The water that dripped through was caught in a container that sat under the hopper. You would then boil the water until grease put in the water would harden (the grease would disappear). This water was your lye. It had to diluted, or it would eat up your hands.

Homemade lye was used to scrub floors and the front and back porches. It would remove grease spots from the kitchen floors. Lye was also used to scrub the wood slats, rope and cane bottoms of chairs. The lye bleached the wood and made it pretty and white.

OUR CLOTHES

Most of our clothing was handmade; all our summer underwear (men and women), dresses and men's work shirts. We had 2 woolen dresses in winter that had to be cleaned in gasoline and ironed with a cool iron on the wrong side.

I remember a Navy blue serge skirt pleated on a waist that buttoned in back. The middy blouse was red flannel with a sailor collar trimmed in sutash braid with "store bought trim," an anchor on one elbow and stars in each corner of the collar. My mother never had a "store bought" pattern; they were made from newspapers. She had a sleeve pattern and enough waste pattern for the armholes. The design was copied from the Sears and Roebuck catalog. We were always allowed to help pick the design. She made her own buttonholes that were a piece of art. They didn't look like hog eyes. My father bought her some buttonhole scissors. She thought it was a waste of money, but she soon discovered their usefulness. When I think about it now, I realize how creative my mother must have been, and how pretty our clothes were.

She sat up many Saturday nights until midnight or later with the coal oil lamp on the end of the sewing machine, so we could have new dresses for Sunday. Such loving care! What devotion! Mothers are like that, at least my mother was.

MAKE DO

There were a lot of things we did -- I think you could say to "make do" -- such as turning collars on men's dress shirts. Collars were reversed in order to put the unworn side on the outside.

We made our sheets and pillow cases from 36 inch brown domestic at 5 cents a yard and sometimes on sale for 2 yards for 5 cents.

The sheets had to be pieced down the middle. To keep from puckering when laundered, tear off 1 piece the desired length and pin the first end of this length to first end of the next length. Put the ends together and pin 2 lengths as you go. When the pieces are the same length, tear the remaining end sew both pieces together down the middle. Hem the sides with a narrow hem. Then hem both ends; one a 2 inch hem, the other a 3 inch hem. By using this method, the threads will be going the same way to prevent puckering. After laundering several times with boiling in lye soap, they will bleach out white.

Marie and I embroidered the pillow cases, and my mother embroidered the sheets that were used for bed spreads. The thread was 20 skeins for a dime. The sheets had hand crocheted lace about 3 inches wide on 3 sides. No one dared to sit on the beds. My father, when going to town, would ask if we needed any Pearline (crochet thread).

TWO ROOM SCHOOL

The second school we went to had 2 teachers and only went to the fourth grade. There were no disciplinary problems that I can recall; nobody was sent to the principal's office - no principal.

The 2 teacher school was a public school, and each morning (would you believe) we answered the roll with a Bible verse taught us by our father at the breakfast table enabling us to learn 2 verses, mine and Marie's.

We always ate our meals at home at the same time, and my father offered thanks. He would thank God for his tender and loving care through the past night, and I thought he was saying through the past nine. It took me awhile to get that one figured out.

While attending the upper grades, I don't remember any classmates ever getting into any trouble with the law, which meant no jail sentences or fines, nor do I remember a girl ever having a baby out of wedlock or even a "shotgun" wedding.

"POOR DO" AND "CRUMBLE IN"

Another dish that was put on the table in the spring was made with meal just like mush. It was put in the skillet to fry with butter, salt, pepper and fresh green onions, blades and all. The last ingredient added was 2 or 3 beaten eggs. My brother called it "poor do" - pronounced por do.

Then our supper was supplemented by a dish my brother called "crumble in." It was simply cornbread put in a goblet with milk. The cornbread usually had fresh green onions baked in it with a little cayenne pepper. Let the milk soak up the cornbread and eat with a teaspoon or soupspoon. Try it, you might like it. We still do.

GEORGE A. ROGERS PHILOSOPHY

If you think you're indispensable, take a ride through the cemetery.

If you think you know it all - you do.

Your rights end where the other person's begin.

You shouldn't have to tell those around you that you are a Christian. Your actions should tell them.

Always tell the truth, and you won't have so much to remember.

If you don't learn something every day, you're dead.

Take pride in what you do, and then you'll enjoy it.

If there was something I was concerned about he would say, "Try not to worry; it will look better in the morning." And sure enough, he was right.

If there is the least bit of doubt in something you want to do, don't do it.

I've never been sorry for the things I didn't say -- just the things I did say.

Try to be pleasant. Nobody loves a grouch.

The man who never made a mistake, never did anything.

You can't point an accusing finger at someone without pointing 3 at you.

You can always find something to be happy about.

Love builds; hate burns.

If someone hurt our feelings, our mother, May Rogers, would say, "Just consider the source."

INDEX

BEEF, *continued*

FISH

FRUITS AND VEGETABLES

DESSERTS

DESSERTS, *continued*

DESSERTS, *continued*

COOKIES AND CANDIES

COOKIES AND CANDIES, *continued*

BREADS

SALADS AND SOUPS

SALADS AND SOUPS, *continued*

RELISHES AND PRESERVES

MEMORIES

THELMA ALLEN
PERSONAL APPEARANCES

When her schedule permits, Thelma Allen would like to talk to your group about the writing of her cookbooks, her memories and how-to-start a new business in your retirement years.

Thelma is available for special appearances for your:
- Church group
- Social club
- Civic organization
- In-store promotion
- Radio and television talk show
- Business

SWEET YESTERDAY
FUND RAISING PROGRAM

The "Recipes From Sweet Yesterday" cookbooks are excellent products that can be sold by your group for your fund raising needs.

FOR APPEARANCE AVAILABILITY AND INFORMATION ON OUR FUND RAISING PROGRAM, CONTACT:

Michael Allen
Michael Allen Entertainment
P. O. Box 111510
Nashville, TN 37222
email: michael@sweetyesterday.com

Visit our Web site:
www.sweetyesterday.com

OTHER SWEET YESTERDAY COOKBOOKS

Recipes From Sweet Yesterday
Volume Two
245 recipes
232 pages
Binding: soft cover, plastic comb-bound
ISBN: 0-9668322-1-3

Recipes From Sweet Yesterday
Volume Three
257 recipes
244 pages
Binding: soft cover, plastic comb-bound
ISBN: 0-9668322-2-1

Recipes From Sweet Yesterday
Volume Four
236 recipes
245 pages
Binding: soft cover, plastic comb-bound
ISBN: 0-9668322-4-8

These titles can be ordered
from Sweet Yesterday,
online at sweetyesterday.com,
online at barnesandnoble.com,
and at any bookstore.

You will enjoy hearing
Thelma Allen
tell
her memories in this
"Stories From Sweet Yesterday"
audio cassette.

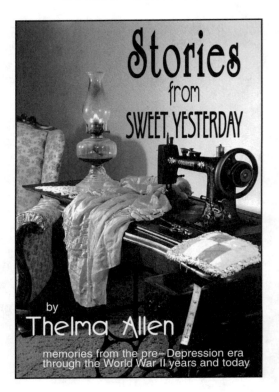

Thelma tells some of the stories from her cookbooks and some new old stories about her pre-Depression days through today on her audio cassette. When she paints word pictures, your imagination will put you back in time.

See order form in this book.

Visit
our Web site
at

www.sweetyesterday.com

- **Free Recipes**

- **Recipe Sharing** (with our Web site visitors)

- **Latest News** From Sweet Yesterday

- Thelma Allen **Personal Appearances**

- Product **News** & Latest **Updates**

    "Recipes From Sweet Yesterday" cookbooks
    "Stories From Sweet Yesterday" audio cassette tape
    New Products

Thanks

for purchasing the

Recipes From Sweet Yesterday

cookbooks.

We know you will enjoy your books.
**You may want to purchase some more copies
for *gifts for friends and relatives!***
Here's a *checklist* for you to use.
Write volume number by name.

● **Order Products** (use order forms on the next pages
or order online with your credit cards)

☐ Birthday gifts for: Date needed:

    (name)_____ _____

    (name)_____ _____

    (name)_____ _____

☐ Wedding gifts for:

    (name)_____ _____

    (name)_____ _____

    (name)_____ _____

☐ Christmas gifts for:

    (name)_____ _____

    (name)_____ _____

    (name)_____ _____

☐ Graduation gifts for:

    (name)_____ _____

    (name)_____ _____

    (name)_____ _____

☐ Mother's Day gifts for:

    (name)_____ _____

    (name)_____ _____

    (name)_____ _____

ORDER EXTRA COPIES
of the
"SWEET YESTERDAY" COOKBOOKS
and the
"STORIES FROM SWEET YESTERDAY" CASSETTE

NO. OF COPIES___**VOLUME 1** @ $10.00 each
NO. OF COPIES___**VOLUME 2** @ $10.00 each
NO. OF COPIES___**VOLUME 3** @ $10.00 each
NO. OF COPIES___**VOLUME 4** @ $10.00 each
NO. OF COPIES___**CASSETTE** @ $10.00 each

SUBTOTAL_____

Add 8.25% sales tax (Tenn. residents only)_____
Postage and handling for 1st book - $4.25_____
    P & H for each additional book - $1.25_____

TOTAL_____

ORDERED BY_____

STREET/APT. NO._____

CITY/STATE/ZIP_____

PHONE (____)_____

MAKE YOUR CHECK OR MONEY ORDER TO: SWEET YESTERDAY.

PLEASE MAIL THIS ORDER FORM WITH YOUR PAYMENT TO:

Sweet Yesterday
P.O. Box 111510
Nashville, TN 37222

Please allow 2 weeks for delivery and always on time for special occasions. All prices are subject to change without notice.

OTHER SWEET YESTERDAY COOKBOOKS

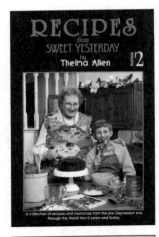

Recipes From Sweet Yesterday
        Volume Two
245 recipes
232 pages
Binding: soft cover, plastic comb-bound
ISBN: 0-9668322-1-3

Recipes From Sweet Yesterday
        Volume Three
257 recipes
244 pages
Binding: soft cover, plastic comb-bound
ISBN: 0-9668322-2-1

Recipes From Sweet Yesterday
        Volume Four
236 recipes
245 pages
Binding: soft cover, plastic comb-bound
ISBN: 0-9668322-4-8

These titles can be ordered
from Sweet Yesterday,
online at sweetyesterday.com,
online at barnesandnoble.com,
and at any bookstore.

ORDER EXTRA COPIES
of the
"SWEET YESTERDAY" COOKBOOKS
and the
"STORIES FROM SWEET YESTERDAY"
CASSETTE

NO. OF COPIES____**VOLUME 1** @ $10.⁰⁰ each
NO. OF COPIES____**VOLUME 2** @ $10.⁰⁰ each
NO. OF COPIES____**VOLUME 3** @ $10.⁰⁰ each
NO. OF COPIES____**VOLUME 4** @ $10.⁰⁰ each
NO. OF COPIES____**CASSETTE** @ $10.⁰⁰ each

SUBTOTAL_____

Add 8.25% sales tax (Tenn. residents only)_____
Postage and handling for 1st book - $4²⁵_____
   P & H for each additional book - $1²⁵_____

TOTAL_____

ORDERED BY_____

STREET/APT. NO._____

CITY/STATE/ZIP_____

PHONE (____)_____

MAKE YOUR CHECK OR MONEY ORDER TO: SWEET YESTERDAY.

PLEASE MAIL THIS ORDER FORM WITH YOUR PAYMENT TO:

Sweet Yesterday
P.O. Box 111510
Nashville, TN 37222

Please allow 2 weeks for delivery and always on time for special occasions. All prices are subject to change without notice.